TALES from the LAND of the SUFIS

TALES from the LAND of the SUFIS

Mojdeh Bayat &
Mohammad Ali Jamnia

SHAMBHALA
Boston & London
1994

SHAMBHALA PUBLICATIONS, INC.
Horticultural Hall
300 Massachusetts Avenue
Boston, Massachusetts 02115

© 1994 by Mojdeh Bayat and Mohammad Ali Jamnia

Title page calligraphy by Mohammad Ali Jamnia: "O Love."

Quotations from William C. Chittick, *The Sufi Path of Love: The Spiritual Teachings of Rumi*,
are reprinted by permission of the State University of New York Press.

9   8   7   6   5   4   3   2   1
First Edition
Printed in the United States of America on acid-free paper   ∞
Distributed in the United States by Random House, Inc.,
and in Canada by Random House of Canada Ltd

Library of Congress Cataloging-in-Publication Data

Bayat, Mojdeh.
Tales from the land of the Sufis / Mojdeh Bayat and Mohammad Ali Jamnia.— 1st ed.
p.   cm. Includes bibliographical references. ISBN 0-87773-955-2 : 1. Sufism—Prayer-
books and devotions.   2. Sufi literature.   I. Jamnia, Mohammad Ali.   II. Title.
BP189.62.B38   1994   297'.43 — dc20   93-39137   CIP

Dedicated to Dr. Javad Nurbakhsh,
Master of the Nimatullahi Sufi Order

CONTENTS

CONTENTS

ACKNOWLEDGMENTS

The authors wish to express their appreciation and gratitude to Kendra Crossen and June Rouse for their invaluable help and support in editing this work. We also wish to thank and acknowledge Dr. Alireza Nurbakhsh, editor of *Sufi: A Journal of Sufism*, and Guy Spiro, editor of the *Monthly Aspecterian*, for encouraging us and publishing the first articles that eventually led to the writing of this book.

TALES FROM THE LAND OF THE SUFIS

INTRODUCTION

Stories and legends are inherent in the mystical tradition of Islam known as Sufism. In this book we wish to introduce the reader to some of the best tales that have been told by famous masters or that describe these legendary Sufis.

In writing this book, we kept two principal considerations in mind. First, we wanted our translations or retellings to reflect the simple quality of the original language. The original Persian texts were written in uncomplicated forms of prose and poetry, so that the stories could be enjoyed by a large group of people. While the stories we present here are based on famous works, in some we have included traditional variations and changes. For example, Attar's story "This Too Shall Pass" originally consisted of only a few lines of poetry. What we bring you here is the fuller folkloric version.

Our second consideration was to accompany the tales with biographies of the original writers in order to convey the character of the storytellers. In becoming acquainted with the tellers of the tales, the reader can develop a more personal understanding of each of them, as well as enjoy the stories for the messages they convey. Thus, each chapter devoted to a Sufi writer begins with a biography of the tale-teller; in the cases of the first two writers—Hallaj and Abu Sa'id—we have portrayed them as legends simply because they are considered to be just that.

After giving a brief history of Sufism in chapter 1, we devote chapter 2 to Hallaj, the legendary Muslim martyr of the ninth and tenth centuries who uttered the words, "I Am the Truth," and was executed on grounds of heresy. His life story was so dramatic that the poet Attar chose it as the subject of one of his books. The lessons Hallaj taught have provided pedagogical material for many a Sufi master who came after him.

Chapter 3 tells the life story of Abu Sa'id, who lived in the northeastern part of Iran in an era of constant political and religious turmoil after a series of wars that had devastated the country. His message of love and kindness brought a measure of sanity to the people, and his fame reached as far as eastern Spain.

Attar is the subject of chapter 4. His *Conference of the Birds* is among the earliest texts written about the Sufi path and the stages of spiritual development.

Chapter 5 is devoted to Nizami of Ganje, who recast in poetry two of the oldest and most famous love stories, one of Arabic origins and the other from the Persian tradition.

Chapter 6 is about the life of Rumi and his master, Shams. Rumi is probably the most celebrated poet of the Middle East and certainly one of the world's greatest poets of mystical love.

Chapter 7 is about Jami, who, like Nizami, put into verse many traditional love stories as a means of introducing the concept of Divine Love. His most famous work, *Yusuf and Zulaykha,* has been translated into many languages.

Broadly speaking, there are three types of Sufi stories: those dealing with one's relationship to oneself and one's personal growth; those dealing with one's relationship to society and other people; and those dealing with one's relationship to God. All three types fall under the general heading of "teaching stories." Although the stories may seem to be quite simple, their deeper significance may, depending on the student's level of understanding, be subtle and very difficult to grasp.

A brief tale such as the following illustrates something of the teaching function of these stories. Once someone asked a shaykh who was sitting among a group of his dervishes what he understood of Sufism. He replied that all he understood was where to sit to get the first cup of tea. Some of the dervishes laughed at this response because they thought it funny, while others were silent because they did not see the humor in it. Only a few understood the teacher's implied message. The hidden key to this puzzling remark is the fact that traditionally the teacher is always served first. Those who become teachers do so after years of hard work and patience. The shaykh's reply can therefore be interpreted to mean that he understood Sufism to be the result of years of hard work.

Once having been initiated and begun the spiritual journey, one often comes across difficulties and roadblocks. It is generally at this time that the spiritual guide tells a story in which the seeker finds similarities between his or her situation and the point of the story. Eventually the seeker learns the proper means of dealing with roadblocks by putting to use what he or she has learned from the story. As a result, stories perform a very subtle yet important function in the training and education of wayfarers on the path.

If a teacher were to confront a pupil directly about what was blocking the pupil's progress, the teacher would likely activate the pupil's defense mechanism. The student's ego would be bruised, and the student would tend to argue that his or her actions were justified. Through the use of stories, the teacher ensures that the ego will not be alarmed and that the lessons will penetrate deep into the psyche.

Thus, stories can serve to increase mental flexibility. The follower learns to give up his or her own perceptions of how things are or ought to be, and become prepared to receive higher levels

3

of training. In fact, there is a saying that a master will not begin to transmit spiritual knowledge to any disciple who displays the slightest sign of self-will.

Not all the stories associated with Sufism require a great deal of contemplation. Many stories are used to convey messages of loving care or to teach particular codes of conduct. If the pupil is ready to cross a barrier, a properly timed story gets the message across; if his attachment to the particular object of the lesson is too great, the student simply does not get the point and his training is not jeopardized. One such story is related by Dr. Javad Nurbakhsh, head of the Nimatullahi Order. It might be used to teach others to see goodness in the ugly things in life:

> One day, Jesus and some of his disciples were walking in an alley when they came across a dead dog. The dog's body had been torn; it had rotted and the odor filled the air. Seeing this, the disciples started complaining about the smell, the sight of the corpse and how ugly the scene was. At that point, Jesus noticed that the dog had unusually bright and clean white teeth. He praised the teeth and pointed them out to his disciples.[1]

Obviously, the point of this story is not to appreciate every dead dog one might come across, but to maintain a positive outlook on life's events. The true meaning of the story is revealed only when we consider the whole picture (the behavior of a perfect man) in relation to the details (an unpleasant and ugly sight).

Other Sufi stories, like the following, deal with the dervishes' conduct in society. Mawlana Abu Sa'id was a great Sufi who lived some nine hundred years ago in northeastern Iran. One day, when he and some of his disciples were passing through an alley, a dog bit the robe of one of them. The one who had been bitten struck the dog with his walking staff. The dog then went to Abu Sa'id and complained about what had happened. Abu Sa'id replied by inviting the dog to bite him in payment for the dervish's improper act of hurting another being. The dog replied that the judgment was not fair because, having seen the man in a dervish's garment, he thought that he could bite at the garment freely, without fear of being beaten. Had the man been wearing the cloak of the common people, the dog would have moved far away from his path. The dog maintained that the proper settlement was to take the dervish's cloak away from him so that no one else could be fooled by it.

Clearly, this story indicates that a Sufi does not retaliate against the hostile actions of others. In fact, this is very similar to Jesus' saying that if someone strikes you on the right cheek, you should turn to him the other also.

Another type of Sufi story deals with the dervish's relationship with, and his journey toward, God. Attar has related several stories of this nature in which a disciple undergoes many harsh and seemingly unrelated calamities, only to discover that the calamities were tests of his sincerity in wanting God.

A large number of Sufi stories have what appear to be sad endings, in which the protagonist either dies or does not complete his or her quest and thus appears to fail. One also encounters stories in which the hero causes harm to an innocent third party for the sake of a lesson or to achieve a goal. These themes are often puzzling or even repugnant to Westerners and thus need clarification in light of the culture from which the stories come.

Perhaps because of the history of the United States, Americans in particular are accustomed to stories with happy endings. (Even when a tale is sad, the ending usually offers some kind of resolution or reconciliation.) In the last three hundred years, there has never been a calamity that has devastated the United States to the extent that it has scarred the psyche of the entire society. The people as a whole have experienced victory; thus, it is natural for them to expect victory also in the stories they read. In fact, Americans basically associate death with defeat. Traces of this mode of thinking can be found in expressions such as "knock 'em dead," which is sometimes used to encourage a sports team to win or to wish someone success in a job interview. It is interesting that no one who says this actually envisions a battle or war being fought, yet for someone to be successful—a "winner"—the opposite party has to be the loser and thus "dead"!

In Persia and the Arab Middle East, by contrast, calamities have at times lasted for centuries. Wars, famines, and unrest have left extremely deep scars on the psyche of the people. Death and dying are not always associated with defeat. In certain circumstances death may signify the highest levels of freedom and accomplishment. Being defeated is recognized as an inevitable part of life and means only that the approach to one's aim was not proper.

It is interesting to compare the meaning of the word *martyr* with its Persian equivalent, *shahid*. Our English dictionary defines *martyr* as "one who is put to death or endures great suffering on the behalf of any belief." But in a Persian dictionary, *shahid* is defined as "one whose knowledge encompasses every thing; one of God's names; witness; being killed for the sake of God." Here, in a subtle way, one can recognize the different connotations of death in the two cultures.

In Sufi literature, "sad" endings reflect such influences. Thus, readers do not really consider the endings sad or at odds with the story line; instead, they understand them as pointing to very important ideas. The most simple of these ideas is that the death of the body does not signify the end of life. Consciousness is seen as being on a journey with a definite goal, and what is called life is only "overnight lodging." Furthermore, from a Sufi point of view, real life begins when one spiritually achieves *baqa'*—unity with God and birth into the world of Truth and Eternity. This unity can be achieved only through *fana'*—the death of worldly desires and selfishness.

The other theme that may be misunderstood by Westerners is

the apparent failure of the hero or heroine to act ethically. In certain stories of Rumi and Attar, for example, there does not seem to be much value given to a human being's welfare. For example, the hero comes to the aid of someone who is in love with a fair maiden. The reader expects that in the end, the lover and the beloved will be united with the help of the hero. But that is not always the case. In one story by Attar, for instance, the hero poisons the maiden to make sure the two will never be together. In situations such as these, one has to bear in mind that in Sufi literature, any beloved other than God is not acceptable; thus, romantic love or love for earthly possessions must ultimately turn into love of God. In the eyes of a seeker, therefore, the object of romantic or worldly love would need to die. What might seem like treachery and evildoing must be looked at in light of the lesson it teaches.

One matter of particular concern to English-speakers these days is the predominance of masculine nouns and pronouns in most traditional literature. Many readers, writers, and editors prefer to use more inclusive language in place of terms such as *man, mankind,* and the pronouns *he* and *him* when used generically—all of which are considered sexist. Islamic culture and Sufism do, of course, reflect a masculine bias in many ways. It may help to know, however, that when it comes to traversing the spiritual path, Sufism regards the two sexes as equal. One of the ways in which this is indicated is the use of the term *brothers* to refer to both male and female aspirants. Thus, both women and men who are true lovers of God are in a sense "men," for in Sufi symbolism, "woman" stands for one who pursues worldly desires. Many Sufi poets and writers, such as Attar and Rumi, have portrayed women characters in their stories in this symbolic context, without intending to insult the female sex. In relation to sexism in English usage, it is also pertinent to note that in the Persian language, Farsi, all pronouns are in the neuter gender, so the problem of whether to use "he" or "she" really only arises in translation.

Because Sufism and Persian culture are so closely associated and intertwined, these various cultural idiosyncrasies are taken for granted by most Persians and do not cause them great concern. We encourage other readers, who may be unfamiliar with the ways of the Middle East, to be open to appreciating these subtleties, and hope that they will find the stories both rich in meaning and enjoyable to read.

A BRIEF LOOK AT THE HISTORY
OF SUFISM

SUFISM is a spiritual system that has had a tremendous impact
on world literature and has affected many cultures, from south-
ern and eastern Europe to northern and central Africa, from the
Middle East to the western frontiers of China. The impact of Sufism on Islamic culture can readily be detected. The design of many
buildings and the architecture in general, the patterns of poetry
and music, and the visual effects of colors and calligraphy are all
areas of Sufi influence in the Middle East.[1] Perhaps less well known
is the fact that concepts such as romantic love and chivalry were
adopted by the West when Europe came into contact with the
Sufis. Moreover, many works of Western literature find their roots
in Sufi stories. The Swiss legend of William Tell, for instance, is
based on Attar's *Conference of the Birds*; and, as Cervantes himself
admitted, *Don Quixote* has Sufi origins.[2]

Scholars have differed on the exact origin of the word *Sufi*. The
majority have agreed, however, that it comes from the Arabic word
suf, meaning "wool," and refers to an individual who wears woolen
clothing. Legend has it that both Moses and Jesus wore wool, and
that about seventy of the disciples of Muhammad, the Prophet of
Islam, wore wool. Why wool? Perhaps there was no particular reason except that wool was extremely cheap. However, since coarse

wool is very uncomfortable when worn over bare skin, the wearing of wool may have represented a renunciation of the material world and physical comfort.

The words *Sufi* and *Sufism* (in the languages of Islamic people) did not come into usage until 150 years after Muhammad. Up to this time, strict observance of the Divine Law (Shari'a, the rules of conduct set forth by Muhammad) was considered to be the only way to achieve salvation. The mystics spent their lives fasting and praying in solitude, away from society. The majority of them seemed to be more concerned with the fires of hell and the fruits of heaven than with reaching God. Although there were masters to help and guide others, the concept of an order or school had not yet come into existence.

Eventually, around 800–850 C.E., the spiritual masters reached a point at which they began to advocate practices for attaining salvation, practices apparently different from the prayers prescribed by the Divine Law. The new practices generally included *zikr* (literally "remembrance," the chanting of God's names and attributes) and participating in regular meetings and activities over and above what was specified by the religious laws. The masters of this era (and the ones who came later) considered the study of Shari'a to be the basic schooling that was needed in order for an individual to enter the university of higher spiritual education. This secondary education was called Tariqa (the Path). It was generally believed that Tariqa was a middle level connecting Shari'a and Haqiqa (Truth or enlightenment), and that the Divine Law, in and of itself, was not sufficient to allow the seeker to realize the Truth.

This period, up to about 1450 C.E., may be considered the golden years of Sufism. Notice that the emphasis shifted completely from the fires of hell and the fruits of heaven to the attainment of God. It was during these years that great men such as Ibn 'Arabi, Rumi, Attar, Shah Ni'matullah Wali, and others were born. By about the end of this era, two concepts were well established. The first, the principle regarding the outlook of the Sufis on the world, is known as the Unity of Being (*wahdat-e-wujud*). Ibn 'Arabi was the first master to teach this concept to his disciples. The second was the idea of the chain or order of Sufi masters (*silsila*).

According to the concept of the Unity of Being, existence, including what we refer to as the universe, is a manifestation of God's attributes and, as such, is not separate from Him. Orders or chains of masters provide help and guidance for seekers desirous of reaching God. Many of the orders of Sufism came into existence at this time, primarily branches of a main chain that goes back to Hasan Basri (who was initiated and taught by 'Ali, the Prophet Muhammad's cousin and son-in-law).

These different orders were not established to compete with one another. Many times, a disciple would receive the right to initiate and guide others and then be instructed to move on to a different city and establish a center there. Often, after a few generations, a center started in this way would develop into a new order — or perhaps the people of the region would stop attending and the center would be closed down.

Since anyone could claim to be a Sufi master, it was important for each center to be able to trace its lineage. Many centers traced their lineage to 'Ali. And 'Ali, in turn, was initiated by Muhammad. In fact, there is a Muslim tradition that one night the Prophet Muhammad rose to heaven and was given a *khirqa* (mantle), to be presented to 'Ali as an indication that he was permitted to guide and teach people on the spiritual path. In turn, 'Ali gave four people the same authority: Hasan and Husayn (two of his sons), Komail, and Hasan Basri. In classical Sufism, these four are referred to as the four Pirs, or masters. Most, if not all, of the legitimate orders of Sufism go back to one of these four masters. The order that was cultivated by Hasan Basri is referred to as the Primary Order because the majority of the other chains of masters came from that order.

It is interesting to note that the Sufis consider most of the great figures of the Old and New Testaments as masters of the path. Rumi, for instance, has given numerous accounts of lessons taught by Ibrahim (Abraham), Musa (Moses), Sulayman (Solomon), Isa (Jesus), and others. These individuals were considered by the Sufis to be perfect human beings whose characteristics and qualities reflected God. All of them based their teachings on particular "platforms." For example, before the time of Jesus, these masters of the path guided and helped people from the spiritual platform presented by Moses. With the coming of Jesus, this platform changed to Christianity. It is hardly surprising that the majority of Sufi masters today believe that to follow the Sufi path one must endorse Islam, the platform presented by Muhammad. Yet clearly, once one reaches the destination, the road taken becomes irrelevant.

For the Western reader, the word *Islam* may need some definition. It has its origin in the Arabic root SLM, meaning "to surrender." Thus *Islam* signifies the action of surrendering to God and His will. Unfortunately, owing to events that have taken place in some of the countries in the Middle East, Westerners may associate the words *Islam* and *Muslim* with beliefs that are fundamentalist, unyielding, and, to some extent, violent. It would be a great pity if such stereotypes prevented anyone from appreciating the authentic spiritual path that is Sufism.

It is relatively simple to give a brief account of the history and development of any path of enlightenment. However, once we begin to discuss the path itself, words alone do not suffice. As Rumi puts it, "When it was time to write about Love, the pen was split in half and the paper was torn." Like most other spiritual paths, Sufism is experiential. In a nutshell, it is a path to God through the gateway of the heart, traveled by means of the vehicle of Love. To understand Sufism, then, the language of the heart is needed. Dr. Javad Nurbakhsh has expressed this in the following poem.

Love's Speech

The speech of Love is beyond words and their meanings.
  For Love, there is another language, another tongue.
My rival demands, "Say something of Love!"
  But for a heart that is deaf, what can I do but keep silent?
He whose heart is aware of the lover's world
  hears only the whisperings of Love and Kindness.
Love speaks in a language unknown to ordinary men;
  leave behind their babble with its headaches.
He who denies Love will never grasp this speech;
  nothing we could say would ever move his heart.
In the way of Loving-kindness, there is no talk;
  only the bankrupt chatter behind every door.
Nurbakhsh, from Love's breath your explanation is eloquent,
  Embraced by the heart of every clear-sighted Gnostic.[3]

HALLAJ

The First Martyr of Sufism

HUSAYN IBN MANSUR HALLAJ is probably the most famous Sufi master of the ninth and tenth centuries of the common era (the third and fourth centuries after the Prophet Muhammad). He gained his fame for having spoken the words, "I am the Truth" and, as a consequence, being brutally executed. To the orthodox clergy this death sentence was justified on the grounds of heresy, for exoteric Islam does not accept the notion that a human being can become one with God—and since Truth is one of the names of God, Hallaj had, in effect, proclaimed his own divinity. The mystics contemporary with Hallaj were also appalled by his declaration, because they believed that a Sufi ought never to reveal his inner experiences to others. They felt that Hallaj lacked the capacity to conceal the divine mysteries and that his execution was the result of God's wrath at his having revealed these secrets.

Although Hallaj did not have many supporters among the acclaimed Sufis of his time, almost all the later masters praised him and the lessons he taught. Attar, in his *Memoirs of the Saints*, has given us a large number of legends that surround Hallaj, along with a commentary in which he states, "I am surprised that we accept a burning bush [referring to God's conversation with Moses] saying, 'I am the Lord,' and indeed believe those words to be the word of God Almighty, but we cannot accept Hallaj saying, 'I am the

Truth,' and those be the words of God Himself!" In his epic poem, the *Mathnawi*, Rumi said, "The words 'I am the Truth' are rays of light on Mansur's lips, while 'I am the Lord' coming from Pharaoh is tyranny."

In order to know Hallaj better and to understand what led him to utter his famous words, it is necessary to learn something of his life. But Hallaj is not only a historical character; he is also a legend. Stories about him have kept him alive to the present day. Some people cursed him for what he stood for, while others had only praise for him. Attar devoted the last chapter of his *Memoirs of the Saints* to Hallaj, and a translation of a large portion of Attar's writings on Hallaj is presented later in this chapter.

THE LIFE OF HALLAJ

Hallaj was born in the Arabized town of Tur in the region of Bayda in southeastern Iran in 866 C.E. Contrary to popular belief, he was not an Arab but of Persian descent. His grandfather was a Zoroastrian, and his father was a convert to Islam.

When Hallaj was an infant, his father, a cotton-wool carder, traveled back and forth between Bayda, Wasit, a city near Ahwaz, and Tustar. Considered the textile centers of the time, these cities were located on the western frontiers of Iran, near important centers such as Baghdad, Basra, and Kufa. In those days, Arabs dominated this region, and his family's immigration meant a certain level of cultural uprooting for Hallaj.

At an early age he began studying Arabic grammar, reciting the Qur'an and commentary, as well as theology. By the time he was sixteen he had completed his studies but felt the need to internalize what he had learned. An uncle of his told him about Sahl, a bold and independent mystic who in the uncle's opinion was propagating the true spirit of Islam. Sahl was a mystic of high spiritual station who had become renowned for his Qur'anic exegesis. He believed in strict observance of the tradition of the Prophet and in very harsh ascetic practices such as supererogatory fasts and prayers of some four hundred rak'ahs a day (A rak'ah is a unit of measure of a Muslim's daily prayer; seventeen are required.) Hallaj moved to Tustar to enter the service of this mystic.

Two years later, Hallaj suddenly broke away from Sahl and moved to Basra. It is not clear why he did so (Massignon attributes the move to Hallaj's political connections).[1] Neither are there any accounts of the type of training he had with Sahl. Apparently he was not considered a particularly important disciple, nor did he receive any special form of training or instruction. However, this is not to say that Sahl did not have an impact on him. One look at Hallaj's harsh ascetic practices brings Sahl to mind. When Hallaj entered Basra in 884, he was already at advanced levels of asceticism. There he met 'Amr Makki, who formally initiated him into Sufism. 'Amr was a disciple of Junayd, at that time the most influential of all Sufis.

Hallaj spent eighteen months with 'Amr but ended up leaving him too. Apparently a close colleague of 'Amr's by the name of al-Aqta', who was also a disciple of Junayd, recognized the spiritual capacity in Hallaj and suggested that the latter wed his daughter. Massignon indicates that the marriage might also have had a political basis because of Aqta''s ties. In any case, 'Amr was not consulted on the matter, as custom would have required. This caused a great deal of animosity and not only led to the eventual breakup of the friendship between 'Amr and al-Aqta' but also jeopardized the master-disciple relationship between 'Amr and Hallaj.

Hallaj, feeling he needed help and guidance to deal with this situation, left for Baghdad to spend some time with Junayd, who counseled patience. To Hallaj, this meant to stay away from 'Amr and have a peaceful life with his family and he moved back to his hometown. It is speculated that he then began to receive instruction from Junayd, mainly through correspondence, and continued his ascetic practices.

Six years went by, and in 892 Hallaj decided to go on pilgrimage, or *hajj*, to Mecca. All Muslims are required to undertake this journey at least once in their lives. This, however, was not going to be a simple prescribed hajj but one that would last an entire year, and every day until nightfall was to be spent fasting. Hallaj's goal in choosing such austerity was to purify his heart—to surrender it to the Divine to such a degree that God would fully encompass him. He returned with many new ideas on topics such as divine inspiration, and he debated these ideas with other Sufis, among them 'Amr Makki and possibly Junayd. It is likely that 'Amr turned completely against Hallaj soon afterward. Attar indicates that Hallaj came to Junayd a second time with some questions about whether the mystic should or should not take action to improve society (Hallaj felt that one should, while Junayd believed in being indifferent to this transitory state called life). Junayd would not answer, which angered Hallaj, and he left. In turn, Junayd predicted his fate.

When Hallaj returned to Basra, he began to preach and attracted a large number of disciples. However, his thoughts were going in a direction opposite to his father-in-law's. As a result, their relationship took a turn for the worse, and he was disowned. He moved back to Tustar, along with his wife and brother-in-law, who were still loyal to him. There he continued preaching and had a great deal of success. But 'Amr Makki, who had not forgotten their conflict, dispatched accusing letters to eminent people in Ahwaz, giving Hallaj a bad name. The situation became so bad that Hallaj decided to disassociate himself from the Sufis altogether and instead keep company with the worldly.

Hallaj put away the garment of the Sufis for several years but nevertheless continued searching for God. In 899, he left on his first apostolic journey to the northeastern borders of the country, then turned south, and finally headed back to Ahwaz in 902. On this trip he met the spiritual masters of many different traditions — Zoroastrians and Manicheans, among others. He also became familiar with the terminologies they used, utilizing them in his later works. When he arrived back in Tustar, he resumed preaching. He gave sermons on the secrets of the universe and talked about what his audience kept in their hearts. Thus he was given the nickname Hallaj al-Asrar. (The word *asrar* can mean "secrets" or "hearts," so Hallaj was the Carder of Secrets, or of Hearts, since *hallaj* means "carder"). He attracted a large number of followers. But his unorthodox words frightened certain members of the clergy, and he was denounced as a charlatan.

A year later he made his second hajj, but this time he traveled as a master with four hundred disciples. A large number of legends associated with this particular trip arose concerning Hallaj and his magical, miraculous abilities (some of these will be mentioned in the next section). These fables in turn earned Hallaj the reputation of having made a pact with the *jinn* — demons with hoofed feet and faces like goats. After this trip, he decided to leave Tustar for good and reside in Baghdad, where a group of famous Sufis lived. He made friendships with two of them, Nuri and Shibli.

In 906, he decided to undertake the task of converting the Turks and the infidels. He sailed to western India, went north to the frontiers of the Muslim territory, and then returned to Baghdad. This trip lasted six years and brought him tremendous fame wherever he traveled. The ranks of his followers continued to grow.

The year 913 was the turning point for his spiritual work. In 912 he had set out on his third and final pilgrimage to Mecca. This trip, which lasted two years, ended with his realization of the Truth. It was at the end of 913 that he felt the veils of illusion lifting, leaving him face to face with the Truth. At this moment he uttered, "I am the Truth," in an ecstatic state. This encounter aroused in him the desire to witness God's love for humanity by becoming a "sacrificial lamb." He would be punished not only for every sin that every Muslim had committed, but also for the sins of every human being. He would become a Muslim Jesus. Indeed, he was looking forward to the gibbet.

In the streets of Baghdad, in the marketplace, and in the mosques a strange call was heard: "O Muslims, help me! Save me from God! O people, God has allowed you to lawfully shed my blood—kill me. Then you will be rewarded, and I will come to contentment. I want this accursed one [pointing to himself] to be killed." Then Hallaj would turn to God, saying, "Pardon everyone, but punish me for their sins."

Strangely, these words inspired people to seek reform in their lives and in their communities. The social and political environment of the time had created a great deal of dissatisfaction within the communities and the ruling class. Many called upon the caliph to uphold the duties bestowed on him by God and Islam. Others were looking to reform and change in society itself.

Needless to say, Hallaj had his share of both friends and foes in and out of the caliph's court. The opposition leaders, many of whom were in the ranks of Hallaj's disciples, considered him a messiah and, in hopes of gaining power, tried to use his impact on the people to create unrest. His supporters in the government protected him so that he could help institute social reforms. Overall, a great deal of turmoil was created, and a dramatic end seemed inevitable.

Eventually Hallaj's choice of associates, along with his views on religion, put him on the wrong side of the ruling class. In 918 he was placed under surveillance, and in 923 he was arrested. The advisor to the caliph was among Hallaj's friends, and for a time he managed to divert any attempt to kill him. Hallaj remained in prison for nearly nine years. During this time he was caught in the crossfire between his friends and his enemies. A series of revolts and coups broke out in Baghdad, and he and some of his associates were blamed as the instigators. These events led to a harsh power struggle in the caliph's court. Finally the caliph's vizier, an old enemy of Hallaj's, managed to take the upper hand, and as a show of strength against his opponents, he secured Hallaj's death sentence and ordered his execution.

In no time, Hallaj was flogged before a large group of people and was exhibited on a gibbet with his hands and feet cut off. His decapitation did not take place until the following day, with the vizier himself present for the announcement of the punishment. After the head fell, the body was soaked in oil and burned. The ashes were then taken to a minaret on the shores of the Tigris, where the wind carried them out over the water.

Hallaj thus died in a most brutal way, but he remains immortal in the hearts of those who yearn for what he achieved spiritually. In his own way he showed the seekers of the Truth the steps that the lover has to go through to reach the Beloved.

LEGENDS AND STORIES OF HALLAJ

How did Husayn ibn-Mansur come to be called Hallaj, a name that translates as "carder" (particularly of cotton)? According to Attar, Husayn ibn-Mansur was passing by a cotton warehouse one day and saw a pile of cotton bolls. When he pointed a finger at the pile, the seeds were at once separated from the fibers. He was also given the nickname Hallaj al-Asrar—the "Carder of Hearts," because he had the ability to read people's minds and answer their questions before they asked.

Hallaj was famous for his miraculous powers and abilities. One of his disciples related the following story.

On Hallaj's second hajj, he went to a particular mountain for a retreat along with some of his followers. After dinner, Hallaj mentioned that he was planning to have some sweets. His disciples wondered how this could be, since they had eaten up everything they had brought with them. Hallaj smiled and walked away into the dark of night. A few minutes later he came back with a dish full of warm cakes of a kind unfamiliar to everyone there and asked them all to join him. One disciple, determined to discover the secret by which Hallaj had produced the cakes seemingly from nowhere, hid his share, and when the group had returned from the retreat he looked for someone who could identify the cake for him. A man from Zabid, a faraway city, recognized the pastry as being from his hometown. The astonished disciple realized that Hallaj had indeed produced the cakes by magic. "There is no way anyone but a jinn could have traveled such a great distance in such a short time!" he exclaimed.

On another occasion, Hallaj was crossing the desert with a group of people on their way to Mecca. At one point his companions expressed a wish for some figs, and he pulled a tray of figs out of thin air. Then they asked for some halva. He produced a tray of warm, sugar-covered halva and gave it to them. After eating it, they exclaimed that the sweet was typical of such-and-such a neighborhood in Baghdad and asked him how he had obtained it. His only reply was that to him Baghdad and the desert were the same. Next, they asked for dates. He paused, stood up, and told them to shake his body as they would a palm tree. The people did so, and fresh dates began to fall from his sleeves.

Hallaj was famous not only for his powers but also for his austerities. At the age of fifty, he said that he had chosen not to follow any particular religion but to take from each whatever practice was most difficult for his *nafs* (ego). He never missed the daily prayers, and with each prayer he made a complete bodily ablution.

At the beginning of his ministry, he owned an old and worn cloak that he had had about him for years. One day it was taken away forcibly, and it was noticed that a large number of insects had nested in it—one of which weighed half an ounce. On another occasion, as he was entering a village, people saw a large scorpion following him and wanted to kill it. He stopped them, saying that the scorpion had been a companion of his for twelve years. He seems to have been quite oblivious to pains of the flesh.

Hallaj's asceticism was his means of reaching God, with Whom he developed a very special relationship. One day, in Mecca at the time of pilgrimage, he saw people in prostration, praying. He, too, put his head to the ground, saying, "O You, the Guide of those who are lost, You are above and beyond the praise of those who praise You and the description that they give of You. You know that I am incapable of showing proper gratitude toward Your benevolence. Do this in my place, for that is the only proper appreciation."

The story of his arrest and eventual execution is particularly touching. One day he said to his friend Shibli that he had been busy with an immense task that would lead only to his death. By the time he had become famous and word of his miraculous powers had spread, he had attracted a large number of followers and had made just as large a number of enemies. Finally the caliph himself found out that he had uttered the heretical words, "I am the Truth." Hallaj's enemies urged him to say instead, "*He* is the Truth." His only reply was, "Yes—everything is He! You say that Husayn [Hallaj] is lost. Of course he is. But the Ocean that covers all is not."

Years earlier, when Hallaj was studying under Junayd, he was told to be patient and quiet. But Hallaj was too much of a maverick to listen, and he left. A few years later he came back to Junayd with questions. Junayd's only reply was that it would not be long before he would redden the gibbet with his blood. Now, it seemed, this prediction was coming true.

Junayd was asked whether Hallaj's words could be interpreted in a way that would save his life. Junayd replied, "Let him be killed, for now is not the time for interpretation." Hallaj was sent to prison.

On the first night of his imprisonment, his jailers came to look for him, but to their surprise, his cell was empty. The second night, not only was Hallaj missing, but the prison itself had vanished! The third night, things were back to normal. The guards demanded, "Where were you the first night? And what happened to you and the prison the second night?" He replied, "On the first night I was in the presence of His Majesty [God], so I was absent here. On the second night, His Majesty was here, so both I and the prison were absent. On the third night, I was sent back!"

A few days before his execution, he found himself in the company of some three hundred prisoners who were confined along with him, all chained. He told them that he would free them all. They were amazed that he was talking only of their freedom and not of his own. He said to them, "We are in God's chains here. If we wished to do so, we could break all the links!" Then he pointed to the chains, and the links opened. The prisoners then wondered how they could escape, since the doors were locked. He pointed a finger again, and openings appeared in the walls.

"Aren't you coming?" they asked.

"No, there is a secret that can be revealed only on the gibbet!" he replied.

The following day, the jailers asked him what had happened to the other prisoners. He replied that he had set them free.

"Why didn't you go?" they asked.

"His Majesty has blamed me, so I have stayed for my punishment," he answered.

The caliph, hearing of this conversation, thought that Hallaj was going to make trouble, so he ordered, "Either kill him or beat him until he recants!" Hallaj was whipped three hundred times with a bundle of switches. With every strike, a voice from the unseen cried out, "Have no fear, son of Mansur." The Sufi master Shaykh Saffar later said, recollecting that day, "I believed in the execution-er's faith more than Hallaj's. The executioner must have had some strong beliefs in executing the Divine Law, for the voice could be heard so clearly, and yet his hands were ever-steady."

Hallaj was taken to be executed. A hundred thousand people had gathered, and as he gazed at the crowd, he cried out: "*Haqq, haqq, haqq, ana'l-haqq*" — "Truth, Truth, Truth, I am the Truth."

At that time, a dervish asked Hallaj to teach him about Love. Hallaj said the dervish would see Love that day, the next day, and the day after that. Hallaj was killed that day; the second day his body was burned, and the third day his ashes were scattered to the wind. Through his very death, Hallaj demonstrated that Love means suffering for the sake of others.

As he walked to the execution site, he strutted with great pride.

"Why do you walk so proudly?" people asked.

"I am proud because I am walking to my slaughterhouse!" he said. Then he sang:

My Beloved takes no blame.
He gave me wine and lavished much attention upon me, like a
    host caring for a guest.
After some time had passed, He called for a sword and the
    execution mat.
This is the reward for those who drink old wine with an old lion
    in the heat of summer.

When he was taken to the platform to be pinned to the gibbet, he willingly climbed up the ladder himself. Someone asked about his *hal* (spiritual state, inner emotions). He replied that the spiritual journey of heroes begins at the top of the gibbet. He made his prayer and walked to the top.

His friend Shibli was present there and asked, "What is Sufism?" Hallaj answered that what Shibli saw was the lowest step of Sufism.

"Whatever can be higher?" Shibli exclaimed.

"I am afraid you have no way of knowing that!" Hallaj replied.

When Hallaj was on the gibbet, Satan came to visit him and

asked, "You said 'I' and I said 'I.' Why is it that you received God's eternal mercy and I, eternal damnation?"

Hallaj replied, 'You said 'I' and looked at yourself, whereas I distanced myself from the self. I gained mercy and you, damnation. Thinking of the self is improper, and separating from the self is the best of good deeds."

The crowd had been throwing rocks at Hallaj. Yet when Shibli threw a flower at him, Hallaj, for the first time, gasped in pain. Someone asked, "You did not show any sign of pain from the rocks, but a flower bothered you. Why?"

He replied, "Those who are ignorant have an excuse. It is difficult to see Shibli throw because he knows he should not."

The executioner then cut off his hands. Hallaj laughed and said, "It's easy to cut off the hands of a man who is bound, but it takes a hero to cut off the hands of all those attributes that separate a man from God." (In other words, leaving the world of multiplicity and coming into union with God takes an extraordinary amount of effort.) The executioner next cut off his legs. Hallaj smiled and continued, "I traveled on earth using these legs. I have others for traveling both worlds. Try cutting those if you can!"

Hallaj then rubbed the stumps of his hands over his face so that both his face and arms were bloodied. "Why did you bloody your face?" people asked. He replied that since he had lost a lot of blood and his face had turned pale, he stained his cheeks with blood lest people think he was afraid to die.

"Why, then," they asked, "did you bloody your arms?"

He said, "I am making ablution. For in Love's prayer there are only two rak'ahs, and it requires an ablution made with blood."

The executioner then took Hallaj's eyes. The spectators screamed. Some were crying and others cursing. Then his ears and nose were cut off.

The executioner was about to cut out his tongue when he asked for a second to say something. "O God, do not turn these people away from You for the work they are doing for You. Praised be the Lord that they cut off my limbs for Your sake, and if they cut off my head it is because of Your majesty." He then quoted from the Holy Qur'an: "Those who do not believe in the Day of Judgment are in a hurry to see it, but the believers are cautious because they know it is true." His last words were: "For those who are in ecstasy, the one and only Beloved is enough."

His mutilated body, which still showed signs of life, was left on the gibbet as a lesson to others. It was not until the next day that the executioner finally cut off the head. While he was doing so, Hallaj smiled and died. People screamed, but Hallaj had shown how truly happy and content he was with the will of God. Every part of his body began to cry out: "I am the Truth." At the time of his death, every drop of his blood that fell on the ground formed the name Allah.

The following day, those who had conspired against him decided that even the cut-up body of Hallaj would cause them trouble, so the order came to burn it. Yet even the ashes cried, "I am the Truth."

Hallaj had foreseen the events of his death and had told his servant that when his ashes were cast into the Tigris, the water level would rise so high that all of Baghdad would be in danger of drowning. He had instructed his servant to take his cloak to the river at that time to calm the waters. When on the third day his ashes were spread by the wind out across the water, the water caught fire and the words "I am the Truth" could be heard. The water began to rise, and the servant did as he had been told. The water level went down, the fire subsided, and Hallaj's ashes were silent at last.

An eminent figure of the time said that he had prayed all night under the execution platform and that at the break of dawn he had heard a voice from the unseen say, "We shared with him one of

Our secrets and he did not keep it. Verily, this is the punishment for those who tell Our secrets."

Shibli mentioned that one night afterward he saw Hallaj in a dream and asked him, "How is God going to judge these people?" Hallaj replied that those who knew he was right and supported him did so for God's sake. And those who wanted to see him dead were ignorant of the Truth and therefore wanted his death for God's sake. So God would have mercy on both groups; both groups were blessed.

- 3 -

Abu Sa'id

The Patron of Sufi Music, Song, and Dance

O NE of the greatest Sufi masters of the tenth and eleventh
centuries was Abu Sa'id Abul-Khayr of Mayhana (one of the
ancient cities of the old province of Khurasan). Dr. A. Zarinkub in
his book *The Value of the Sufi Heritage* writes that this master, whose
stories of miraculous powers have taken exaggerated proportions,
had gathered a very large number of followers and believers. But
his boldness of character and indulgence in *sama'*—the ecstatic
dancing and reciting of poetry—aroused a great deal of animosity
among religious scholars and scientists. This eventually led to a
number of assassination plots against him, which were, fortunately,
unsuccessful.

To understand Abu Sa'id, it is necessary to take a brief look at
the esoteric and exoteric sciences of the time. In the ninth century
(about a hundred years before Abu Sa'id's time), during the Abas-
sid caliphate, many Greek and Indian books on the natural sciences, philosophy, and logic were translated into Arabic, revolu-
tionizing the way Middle Eastern scholars approached their
particular fields. Owing to this influx of learning (whether directly
or indirectly), many religious scholars of various denominations
began to discuss Islamic Law and its implications. The esoteric
"scientists"—that is, the mystics of Islam—were also affected, in
that their emphasis on piety and austerity very slowly gave way to

a stress on Gnostic thinking, which represents a much more internal approach to spiritual life. For instance, Junayd considered pious adherence to the external regulations of religion, prayer, and ascetic practices to be of lower value than the contemplation of God's Unity. As he once said, "The best gatherings and the highest seats are where there is contemplation on the circle of Unity."[1]

Another change that took place around this time was the increased use of poetry in expressing the deep inner emotions and spiritual states of the mystic. Up until then, the Sufi masters had not paid any attention to poems (with a few exceptions; some masters such as Hallaj recited poetry when they were in ecstatic states). Even in the province of Khurasan, the center of Persian literature at the time, poetry was not the tool of expression in Sufism. Abu Sa'id, however, was a strong advocate of poetry. He had memorized some thirty thousand lines of verse even before he became an initiate of the Sufi path. As a teacher and a Sufi master, he used poetry in two distinct ways. First, he recited it at Sufi gatherings and *sama‘* sessions to increase the intensity of the ecstatic state. At one gathering that Abu Sa'id attended, the *qawwal* — a singer of spiritual songs in which the Beloved is addressed in a most intimate manner — sang the following verse:

I will hide in my song
So that I may take kisses from your lips as you sing it.

Abu Sa'id was so profoundly affected that he decided to visit the tomb of the poet who had penned those lines and pay his respects.

Poetry also helped Abu Sa'id to teach and guide his disciples. Although the best examples of instructive Sufi poetry can be found in the works of Sana'i, Attar, and Rumi, it was Abu Sa'id who first used poetry for this purpose.

Perhaps the most important contribution of Abu Sa'id to Sufism was the establishment of Sufi centers, or *khanaqahs*, as formal training halls for spiritual training, as well as the development of rules of conduct for the dervishes. The code of chivalry that he founded is followed to this day by the traditional Sufi orders of the Middle East.

Of the large number of books that have been written about Abu Sa'id over the centuries, all but two have been destroyed or lost. The two survivors are *The Secrets of Unity in the Stations of Shaykh Abu Sa'id* and *The States and Words of Abu Sa'id*. Both were written by his descendants about a hundred years after his time. They constitute a collection of stories involving Abu Sa'id or anecdotes related to him and serve as a mirror of the history of his times.

ABU SA'ID'S LIFE AND TEACHINGS

Abu Sa'id Abul-Khayr was born in 978 C.E. in the city of Mayhana in northeastern Iran and died in the same city in 1061. Today nothing is left of this ancient city but his tomb and the building that houses it. However, Mayhana was at one time one of the more important cities of the old province of Khurasan.

Abu Sa'id's father was a pious adherent of orthodox Islam, yet he was also familiar with the Sufi path. On many occasions he used to attend Sufi gatherings for *sama'*. One time, Abu Sa'id's mother persuaded his father to take the boy along in hopes that the grace of the Sufis might benefit him. There the *qawwal* chanted the following quatrain:

> God gives the dervishes Love—and Love is woe;
>> By dying near and dear to Him, they grow.
> The generous youth will freely yield his life;
>> The man of God cares naught for worldly show.[2]

This song moved the dervishes deeply, and they danced to it all night long. The *qawwal* sang it so often that Abu Sa'id learned it by heart. When he and his father returned home, he asked his father what the quatrain meant. His father responded harshly that Abu Sa'id would not understand and that it was none of his concern.

Years later Abu Sa'id recalled this incident and concluded that it was really his father who did not understand the poem—which expresses the basic Sufi teaching that to unite with God, who is Love itself, the aspirant must be willing to allow his or her self to be annihilated.

Apparently, the divine fire of love was alive in Abu Sa'id since childhood. An event took place in his early years that made his father sit up and notice his son's potential. Abu Sa'id's father, an admirer of King Mahmud, had built a new house with murals portraying the king in luxurious surroundings on its walls. Upon seeing the murals, Abu Sa'id asked his father for a room of his own. Once his wish had been granted, Abu Sa'id painted the word *Allah* on his walls. When questioned by his father about why he had done this, he replied, "Everyone writes the name of his king on the walls of his house." Amazed at the boy's clever way of reminding him that God alone is King, the father gave orders to have all the murals of King Mahmud removed from the house.

This incident with Abu Sa'id affected his father greatly, and he decided to do what he could to educate his son. At first Abu Sa'id was sent to Abu (or Bu) Muhammad Anazi (or Ayari) to study the basics of the Qur'an and grammar. It is not clear how long he studied with Abu Muhammad. However, one Friday as he and his father were going to pray, they came across Pir Bishr Yasin, one of the great sages of the period. At the sight of Abu Sa'id, Pir Bishr became ecstatic and told the boy's father, "We could not have left this world because our seat would have been left empty and the dervishes would have been left alone. Now I can rest assured." Then he asked the two to visit him in his hermitage after the prayer.

When they got to the hermitage, they conversed with Pir Bishr for a while. Pir asked Abu Sa'id's father to lift his son so that he could reach a loaf of bread that was sitting on a high shelf. Years later, when Abu Sa'id was describing this incident, he said, "The loaf was warm to the touch, and when Pir took it from me, he got excited and cried. Then he broke it into two pieces. He ate one piece and gave the other to me. My father was surprised that he was not given a share of this divine grace." Pir told Abu Sa'id's father, "It is now thirty years since I put this loaf on that shelf. I was promised that the person whose touch warms this loaf will give life to the world."

From then on, Abu Sa'id studied under the supervision of both Bu Muhammad and Pir Bishr. He learned the Qur'an and grammar from the former and the principles of Islam from the latter. After he finished his studies of the Holy Book, Pir Bishr taught him the basis of the disinterested love of God—loving the Lord for His own sake, because He alone is worthy of being loved, and not for the sake of rewards or out of fear of punishment.

Later on, Pir asked Abu Sa'id whether he wanted to talk to God.

"Of course I want to."

"Then whenever you are by yourself, recite:

'Without Thee, O Beloved, I cannot rest;
    Thy goodness toward me I cannot reckon.
Though every hair on my body becomes a tongue,
    A thousandth part of the thanks due to Thee I cannot tell.' " [3]

Abu Sa'id later revealed that he repeated this quatrain so many times that a way to God opened to him at an early age.

Pir Bishr soon died, but Abu Sa'id continued studying the exoteric Islam for years, traveling from city to city and from teacher to teacher. His last teacher of the exoteric was Abu Ali Faqih, who lived in the city of Sarakhs. There he studied the science of interpretation of the Holy Book, the principles of Islam, and the traditions of the Prophet. And it was there that he met someone who would change the course of his life.

STEPPING UPON THE PATH

One day, as Abu Sa'id was on his way to see his teacher, he met Luqman, a pious Muslim and a lover of God who had lost his mind. Rumor had it that he had felt he was not doing enough for God, and that the more he did, the less it seemed. Finally, he had asked God to release him from his obligations, and his prayers had been accepted. His madness was a sign of his freedom.

Abu Sa'id, seeing Luqman sitting on a pile of ashes, making something from a lambskin, asked what he was doing. Luqman replied, "I am making your cloak." He then grabbed Abu Sa'id's hands and took him to Pir Abul-Fadhl Hasan's *khanaqah*.

That day, Pir Abul-Fadhl informed Abu Sa'id that 124,000 prophets had come and told people to call on Allah. For some listeners, this admonition went in one ear and out the other. But there were others who listened and began to repeat the name of Allah. These were drowned in their remembrance and were eventually cleansed. Then Allah's name appeared in their hearts, and they no longer needed to repeat it. Abul-Fadhl's words affected Abu Sa'id so deeply that he could not sleep that night.

The next day, after the morning prayer and recitation of the litany, Abu Sa'id went to see his teacher, Abu 'Ali Faqih. The lesson that day was taken from the Qur'anic verse, "Say, 'Allah,' and leave them to amuse themselves in their folly." Upon hearing this verse, Abu Sa'id fell into a state of rapture. He later mentioned that a door had opened in his heart. When Abu 'Ali saw the change in his student and found out where he had been the day before, he expelled him from his class and sent him off to Pir Abul-Fadhl.

After serving Pir Abul-Fadhl for a while, Abu Sa'id was ordered to return to his hometown and find seclusion to "attend to God." Abu Sa'id recounts of this period that he remained seated in the chapel of a hermitage, repeating the words, "Allah, Allah, Allah." Whenever he fell asleep or his mind became cluttered, an ugly demon with a flaming staff would appear and order him to get back to his recitation. Abu Saʿid was so terrified of the demon that he continued to repeat Allah's name until his entire being began to say, "Allah, Allah, Allah."

After this incident, he went back to Pir Abul-Fadhl and began a new series of austerities and hardships. Finally he was fully accepted by Pir Abul-Fadhl and received the Sufi cloak. The lineage of Abul-Fadhl was to Abu Nasr Sarraj, to Abu Muhammad ʿAbdullah, and to Junayd.[4] After Pir Abul-Fadhl's death, Abu Saʿid continued his training and put himself through more hardships. He apparently spent seven years in an arid land, eating the roots of thorny plants. He then traveled to the city of Amul to serve Shaykh Abul-ʿAbbas, whose lineage goes back to Junayd through Tabari and Jariri. He stayed in Amul for one year (some sources say two and a half years) and received a cloak from Shaykh Abul-ʿAbbas as well. The author of *The Secrets of Unity* goes into some detail about this second cloak and says that in receiving a second cloak, Abu Saʿid was not really accepting a different master or path; rather, since the Sufis are one in spirit, the two cloaks were really one and the same. After his time with Shaykh Abul-ʿAbbas, Abu Saʿid returned to Mayhana and Shaykh Abul-ʿAbbas died a short while later.

Abu Saʿid considered Shaykh Abul-ʿAbbas to be a perfect master and an *insan-i kamil*—a complete man, one perfected in love and suffering—but he kept a particularly soft spot in his heart for Pir Abul-Fadhl. This affection was so great that he used to visit his teacher's tomb in Sarakhs whenever he had a mystical experience that he could not resolve or when he experienced a feeling of contraction (*qabd*, or spiritual sadness) in his heart. Once, when he was giving a sermon, he fell into such a state of contraction and began crying. The audience also became sad and started to weep. After this state had continued for some time, he decided to visit Pir Abul-Fadhl's tomb, and upon arriving at the grave, he and all those who had accompanied him felt an expansion in their hearts. Abu Sa'id began to dance and sang the following verse:

> This is the mine of happiness,
> and the mine of mercy;
> Our *qibla* is the sight of the Friend
> and the *qibla* of others is Ka'ba.

This event took place a short while after Abu Sa'id had reached perfection and had given up the harsh ascetic training that he had been following. Now he no longer needed to adhere to strict practices and rituals. His direct vision of God—the Friend—was now his *qibla*, his prayer direction, whereas others still remained attached to the convention of praying in the direction of the Ka'ba in Mecca.

A GUIDE FOR OTHERS

When all the veils of illusion were lifted for Abu Sa'id and he had attained enlightenment, he decided to leave his hometown and go to Nishapur. There is a story that a man by the name of Mahmud, who was very respected by the shaykh, had a dream that the mountain near Nishapur split in half and a full moon came up. The moon traveled through the sky and landed at the *khanaqah* of the Adanykouyan district. From this dream, Mahmud knew that a great spiritual personality was coming to Nishapur, for a perfect lover of God is symbolized by the full moon, which has no light of its own but fully reflects that of the glorious sun (God). The splitting of the mountain meant that no obstacle, however great, could block the path of such a one. Mahmud went outside the city to greet Abu Sa'id and brought him to the *khanaqah* that he had dreamed about.

From that day on, Abu Sa'id gave daily talks and sermons that fascinated people, who gave him their wealth for the *khanaqah* or donated it to the needy at his instruction. His approach was to

35

engage in *sama'* continuously, to recite poetry and lyrics, and to teach people to let go of themselves in order to reach God. He also made it clear that he knew what went on in people's daily lives and private moments. This ability caused the common people to believe in him, and the religious scholars to condemn him.

The scholars of exoteric religion believed that in sermons, only the Traditions of the Prophet, the verses of the Qur'an, and the words of the exoteric saints were to be recited, and that any deviation was heresy. At first they questioned Abu Sa'id's approach, since they considered it wrong. When they realized that he was developing a large following, they tried to stop him, and on several occasions they attempted to murder him and his disciples. Yet Abu Sa'id never seemed to mind his enemies' harsh treatment, and he always dealt with them in a kindly manner.

Two tribal leaders, Abu Bakr Ishaq and Sa'id, both extreme fundamentalists, considered Abu Sa'id a heretic and used every opportunity to stop him. When all else failed, they considered killing him. They wrote to King Mahmud, saying, "A Sufi master has appeared who, instead of reciting from the Holy Book and telling about the Traditions of the Prophet, sings, dances, and recites poetry. For meals, instead of harsh foods, he and his disciples eat broiled chicken and many fine dishes and sweets. This is not the way of the pious. He is up to no good and has caused a large group of people to go astray."

King Mahmud replied that they could deal with this Sufi master in any way that they felt would satisfy Islamic law. In no time the whole city knew about the king's reply. Abu Sa'id's followers among the people were upset because they knew the reply was in fact a death sentence for Abu Sa'id. His close disciples were upset, too, for they wanted neither themselves nor their master to be hanged. But no one dared say anything to Abu Sa'id himself.

A short while before sunset, Abu Sa'id called Hasan, his trusted servant, and asked, "How many dervishes are there in the *kha-naqah*?"

"Eighty guests from other cities and forty who live here. All together a hundred and twenty."

"What are you going to feed them for breakfast?"

"Whatever you command."

"You should serve everyone broiled lamb heads with plenty of sugar and plenty of sweets and rosewater. Moreover, burn some incense. Make sure to set all the food on a clean white cotton cloth in the middle of the city's mosque, so that those who talk behind our backs can see what viands God feeds His elect from the unseen world."

Hasan left for the marketplace with not a cent in his pocket, for there was no money to be had in the *khanaqah*. Once there, he thought he might be able to beg for alms; he was not about to complain to his shaykh about the lack of funds. He stayed at the entrance of the market for a while and saw that people were closing their shops and going home. No one helped him out. He vowed to himself that he would not go back empty-handed, even if he had to stay all night long. It became dark, the market was totally empty, and still no help had arrived. After a few more hours, Hasan saw a man walking toward him. When the man drew closer, he asked Hasan why he was standing there. Hasan told him the whole story. The man smiled, opened a bag, and told him to reach in and take as much money as he desired. Thus Hasan managed to provide all the items that Abu Sa'id had ordered.

The next morning, breakfast was arranged as planned. The shaykh and the dervishes came to eat. The large group of people who gathered to witness the Sufis' fate found them instead eating merrily, seemingly quite unconcerned. Needless to say, the news made its way to Abu Bakr. He replied, "Let them have this last meal; tomorrow they will be food for the vultures."

After breakfast, Abu Sa'id told Hasan to prepare a place for the

Sufis in the first row of worshipers at the Friday prayer. The prayer leader that day was Saʿid, Abu Saʿid's other enemy. Hasan prepared one hundred and twenty places for the Sufis in the first row, and the prayer started. Now, the Friday prayer by custom had two parts: the first was devotional, while the second consisted of a sermon (khutba) given by the prayer leader, usually about social issues. Abu Saʿid completed the devotional portion but did not intend to stay for the lecture afterward. As he was preparing to leave, Saʿid wanted to curse him for not completing the entire prayer, but Abu Saʿid simply turned and stared at him. Saʿid fell silent and remained so until all the Sufis had left. Then he went on with his sermon.

After they had left the mosque, Abu Saʿid instructed Hasan to go to a vendor at the Kermanian crossroads and buy kauk (a type of pastry) and monnagha (a kind of bean), take them to Abu Bakr, and tell him, "Abu Saʿid would like you to break your fast with these."

When Hasan arrived and delivered Abu Saʿid's message and gift of food, Abu Bakr was puzzled at first, then amazed. It so happened that on the same day, Abu Bakr had decided to fast but had not mentioned it to anyone. On his way to Friday prayer, he had passed by the Kermanian crossroads and there had seen some tempting kauk and monnagha on display. But, since he was fasting, he had decided to wait and have the treat for dinner. However, by the time the prayers were done, he had totally forgotten his promise to himself. All this had happened without anyone else being aware of it. When Abu Saʿid had sent him what he wanted, he realized he did not have the strength to fight someone who knew so much about what went on in people's hearts. So after a few minutes, he sent a messenger to Saʿid saying he was not willing to cooperate in killing Abu Saʿid and that Saʿid was on his own.

The messenger returned with a reply from Saʿid in which he described his own encounter with Abu Saʿid, saying that when Abu

Sa'id had looked at him, he had lost all his power. He had felt as if Abu Sa'id were a hawk and he a sparrow. Not surprisingly, he wanted nothing more to do with Abu Sa'id.

As Hasan was preparing to leave Abu Bakr's house, the latter told him, "Say to your master that Abu Bakr with twenty thousand soldiers, Sa'id with thirty thousand men, and King Mahmud with one hundred thousand men and seven hundred war elephants came to fight him, and he defeated them with some sweets and beans. Now we will leave him alone."

Hasan returned to his shaykh and told him the story as it had unfolded. Shaykh Abu Sa'id then told his followers, 'Since yesterday you have been shaking with fear, terrified of being hanged for being a Sufi. Yet it takes someone of the caliber of Hallaj to be hanged — and he has no equal in East or West! Real men are hanged, not phonies." Then he asked the *qawwal* to read out the following poem:

> To the battlefield come prepared
>   with nary a thought of self—just follow us.
> Whether life is like water or fire,
>   Live happily, and in the midst of it be content.

The foregoing story exemplifies Abu Sa'id's approach to his enemies and his custom of returning softness for their harshness. His goal was to clear the path for his followers and to shed light on its darker corners. Many times his friends and disciples would object to his approach or his actions, considering them illogical. Yet they also realized that he always had something to teach them.

There was a Sufi in Nishapur named Abul-Qasim Qushayri who was a moderate follower of the path and who had his own following. When he heard that Abu Sa'id had come to town and that the shaykh's approach to the path was radically different from his own, he at first condemned Abu Sa'id. After a year, however, the two men developed a certain level of friendship. But that did not stop

Abul-Qasim from disapproving of the shaykh's practices of *sama'*
dancing.

One day, Abul-Qasim was passing by the shaykh's *khanaqah* and
saw him and his disciples engaged in *sama'* dancing. The thought
occurred to Abul-Qasim that according to the Law, a man who
dances may not be a witness in court (since he is clearly a madman), and thus justice could not be served. When he ran into Abu
Sa'id on the street the next day, Abu Sa'id asked him, 'When have
you ever seen us in the line of witnesses?" Abul-Qasim immediately
knew that Abu Sa'id was responding to his thought of the day
before. He was ashamed, and vowed not to judge Abu Sa'id in any
way.

A few days later, he again passed by Abu Sa'id's *khanaqah*. He
heard the *qawwal* sing:

> No shame in becoming an idol worshiper
> for the sake of an idol.
> You will not have an idol,
> until you become an idol worshiper.

He saw that Abu Sa'id was dancing in ecstasy. It seemed to him
that in no way could the shaykh be interpreting these lines in any
way other than their literal meaning—the verse was clearly a call
to pantheism, which is anathema to Islam. When he came to visit
the shaykh the next day, Abu Sa'id turned to him and said,

> No shame in becoming an idol worshiper
> for the sake of an idol?
> You will not have an idol
> until you become an idol worshiper?

He then went on to say that the meaning of this verse was that
most people were unashamed to worship what was other than
God, and that in doing so they had become idol worshipers. Upon
hearing this, Abul-Qasim truly understood the high level and station of Abu Sa'id and never again judged him.

Abu Sa'id thus taught Abul-Qasim that there is a monotheism in pantheism if one's eyes are open, and that without such vision, even worshiping God can be considered idolatry. In his explanation of the poem, Abu Sa'id pointed to the fact that most people do not focus on what they are doing, whether it is praying to God or building a house. To focus on one thing to the exclusion of everything else is in itself a form of Unity. Thus, a person who does not focus on any one thing cannot know the true meaning of Unity. (Of course, the highest form of this focus would be concentration on God and His attributes.)

Abu Sa'id used every event as an opportunity to teach. Abdul-Samad, the shaykh's elect disciple, told the following story: "I had been traveling for a while and regretted that I had not been able to attend the shaykh's sermons and enjoy the lessons. When I came back to Mayhana and was again able to attend his sermons, he told me there would be no need to regret what I had missed even if I did not attend his lectures for ten years, because he always says only one thing, and that one thing can be written on a fingernail: 'Sacrifice your ego [nafs], and no more.' "

Abu Sa'id had a newly initiated disciple by the name of Sankani, who came from a well-to-do family. He was young and enjoyed fine clothing and appearances. One day, Abu Sa'id was invited to an outing, and a number of disciples, including Sankani, accompanied him. As they walked, Abu Sa'id was trailing behind and noticed that Sankani seemed preoccupied with his own clothing and fine looks. The shaykh told Sankani not to walk in front of him. Sankani moved behind the shaykh. After a few minutes, Abu Sa'id told him, "Do not walk behind me." So the disciple moved to the shaykh's right. A few minutes later came the request, "Do not walk on my right." Sankani moved to the left, only to find that he was not supposed to be there either. He was perplexed, became upset, and asked the shaykh where he was supposed to be. Abu Sa'id replied that he should drop his ego and walk straight ahead. Then he recited this poem:

> As long as your ego accompanies you, you know naught of God,
> For the ego dislikes the universal man.

The universal man (or "complete man," *insan-i kamil*) removes the veil of the ego from one's eyes so that one can "see" God with God's eyes. Thus, for God to come, the ego must go!

LAST DAYS

At the age of eighty-two, Abu Sa'id left Nishapur for Mayhana, where he gave lectures daily. In each lecture he would predict that there would be a shortage of God in society — that is, that after his death, people would become absorbed in material affairs and ignore spirituality. He lectured for one year, and in his last sermon, he said, "If anyone asks about your identity, do not say that you are believers — Sufis or Muslims; for you will be asked to prove whatever you say. Say instead that you are followers, and that your leaders are elsewhere. Say, 'Ask our leaders, for they will have the answers.' Find out who your spiritual leaders will be, for if you are left to yourselves, much mischief will occur."

Abu Sa'id died in 1061 and was buried in Mayhana. His tomb was maintained by his descendants for about 120 years, after which the invasion of the Turcomans of the Ghuzz tribe began. Some 115 members of the shaykh's family were massacred, and the city itself fell into ruin.

ANECDOTES OF ABU SA'ID

The Bath House

In Abu Sa'id's time, people used public bathhouses very similar to those used today by the Japanese. One day Abu Muhammad, a friend and disciple of the shaykh's, went to visit him at his *kha-naqah*. When he arrived, he was told that the shaykh was at the bathhouse. He immediately went to the bathhouse to look for him. When Abu Muhammad found Abu Sa'id, the shaykh asked him, "Isn't this bathhouse pleasant?"

"It certainly is."

"Why do you think so?"

"Because you have graced this place with your presence!"

"I'm afraid that is not a good reason."

"Would you honor me by giving me the reason?"

"This place is pleasant because one needs no more than a jug to pour water on one's body and a towel to dry oneself with; and those items belong not to the bather but to the bathkeeper."

The Ceremony

One day Abu Sa'id decided to join a religious gathering that was taking place in his city. At the gatherings in those times, it was customary to introduce the guests as they arrived. When the announcer noticed that Abu Sa'id was present, he was at a loss for a proper introduction. He asked the shaykh's disciples, but they were also helpless. Finally, Abu Sa'id heard about the problem. He told the announcer, "Go out and say that Nobody, Son of Nobody, has arrived."

The announcer did so. The eminent and acclaimed people at the gathering were impressed and touched by the high degree of humility that Abu Sa'id had thus shown.

The Dust Ball

A dervish was sweeping the courtyard of the *khanaqah*. Abu Sa'id saw him and said, "Be like the dust ball that rolls before the broom, and not like the rock left behind." With these words the shaykh showed the young disciple that to advance on the path, one must be like the dust, which has no will of its own but goes wherever the broom (the spiritual master) commands—and must not be like the rock (the ego), which asserts its own will and resists the direction of the perfect guide.

Snake

On an outing one day, Abu Sa'id and one of his disciples passed through a region infested with poisonous snakes. As they were walking, a snake slithered close to Abu Sa'id and began to wrap itself around him. The disciple, struck with fear and wonder, stood motionless. Upon seeing the condition of his disciple, the shaykh said, "Do not be frightened. This snake has come to pay his respect and will not harm me. Do you wish him to say hello to you as well?"

"I certainly do!" replied the dervish eagerly.

"That, my friend, will never happen so long as it is your ego that desires it!"

The Old Tamboura Player

At the end of one of the Sufi gatherings, the shaykh and his elect servant, Hasan, were standing at the doors as usual, saying goodbye to those who were leaving. Hasan was preoccupied with thoughts of a sum of money he owed and was worried that he had no means of paying the loan back on time. He was wishing in his heart that the shaykh would give him some advice.

Hasan was brought out of his reverie when he heard Abu Sa'id say, "Look, someone is coming. Go and see what you can do for her." It was an old woman, whom Hasan took inside and offered some tea. The woman then gave Hasan a bag of gold coins to give to the shaykh in exchange for some prayers for her soul.

Happy with the thought that this money might help relieve him of his debt, Hasan took the bag back to Abu Sa'id. To his chagrin, however, he discovered that the money was to be used for another purpose. Abu Sa'id told Hasan to go to the city's cemetery. There, in a corner of the only building there, he would find an old man. Hasan was to wake him up, give him the shaykh's regards, and deliver the coins to him. Hasan did accordingly, and when he gave the old man the gold, the man cried and begged Hasan to take him to Abu Sa'id.

The man told Hasan, "I am a tamboura player. When I was young, I was popular and everybody loved my music. People used to pay me well, and I was constantly invited to celebrations and gatherings. As I grew older, I became less and less popular, and finally nobody wanted me and my music. Eventually, I was thrown out of my own home by my family. I found my way to this cemetery, and now I beg for my food. Last night, I came here tired, hungry, and desperate. I had no one to turn to but God. I wept and prayed and told Him that no one wanted my music. I told Him that I was going to play for Him, in the hope that He would pay me. I played, sang, and cried all night and finally fell asleep near sunrise. And now you have shown up with a bag of money."

Hasan took the tamboura player to the *khanaqah*. Upon seeing Abu Sa'id, the old man dropped to the shaykh's feet, praising God and asking Abu Sa'id to pray for his soul. Abu Sa'id treated him with great kindness, and later told Hasan, "No one has ever lost when he has put his trust in God. Just as the money was provided for this man, it will be provided for you as well."

Don't Be a Storyteller

Khwaja Abdul-Karim, one of the shaykh's elect servants, said, "One day, a dervish asked me to write down some stories about the shaykh's miraculous powers. Shortly thereafter I received word that the shaykh wanted to see me. When I entered the shaykh's room, Abu Sa'id asked me what I was doing. I told him. He then advised me not to be a storyteller but to strive to reach the point where others would tell stories about me." Abu Sa'id knew what his disciple was doing and did not want to become famous for his "powers." He had seized the moment to teach yet another lesson.

Miraculous Powers

One day, Abu Sa'id was told that a certain person could walk on water. He replied, "That is simple; a frog and a mosquito can also walk on water." Then he was told that another man could fly. He replied, "That, too, is simple; a fly and a raven can also fly." Finally he was told about someone who could go from one city to another in the wink of an eye. He replied, "Satan can go from east to west in one breath. These abilities have no value whatsoever. A true human being is one who can mix and socialize with people but does not forget to remember God for even a moment."

The Mill

Abu Sa'id was traveling with his companions when they came across a mill. He stopped his horse and listened to the sound of the mill. Then he asked. "Do any of you know what the mill is saying?" They all shook their heads. He said, "It is saying, 'Sufism is what I have. I receive the coarse and give it back fine. I travel around myself and in myself so that I dispel what I do not need.'"

Elegance

The shaykh's disciples asked him to identify the most elegant man of the city. His choice was Luqman. This surprised them, because Luqman was the town's madman: he had long, uncombed hair, rough clothing, and a harsh appearance. "Remember that *elegant* means 'cleansed.' and *cleansed* means 'not attached or tied to anything,' " said Abu Sa'id. "There is no one in this city cleaner, and with fewer attachments and ties, than Luqman."

Service

One day, in the middle of a talk, Abu Sa'id said, "There are jewels spread all over the *khanaqah*. Why are you not collecting them?"

His audience began to look around, but nobody could find a single one. "We do not see any jewels," they said.

"Serve, serve. That is what I mean!"

The Way of Reaching God

One day a man asked the shaykh about the ways of reaching God. "The ways to God," he replied, "are as many as there are created beings. But the shortest and easiest is to serve others, not to bother others, and to make others happy."

FARIDUDDIN ATTAR

The Divinely Inspired Storyteller

"THE world is like a caravanserai with two doors: entering by one door, you pass out through the other. You are sunk in heedless sleep and know of nothing; you shall die whether you will it or not. Be you beggar or king . . . willy-nilly you must in the end be parted from all that you have. Though you be an Alexander, this transitory world will one day provide a shroud for all your Alexander-like glory."[1] These are the words of Fariduddin Attar, a Persian mystical poet and Sufi master who lived in the twelfth century C.E.

For centuries, Attar's poetry has influenced seekers on both Eastern and Western mystical quests, yet his work is not widely known in the West. Attar, the author of *The Conference of the Birds* and over a hundred other texts, has been a model for many of the celebrated Sufi masters, notably Jalalaluddin Rumi, the greatest of all Sufi poets and the founder of the Order of Whirling Dervishes. Westerners are generally much more familiar with Rumi, since most of his works have been translated into English and other European languages, and commented upon by prominent scholars. Yet Rumi, an acknowledged genius of the mystical world, said, "All I have said about the Truth, I have learned from Attar."

Attar is thus one of the most important Sufi figures. He brought new light to the teachings by explaining the path through the art of storytelling, in a way that no one had done before him. His poetry is still recited among contemporary Sufis, and his stories are told among the laypeople. Rumi said of him, "Attar traversed the seven cities of Love, and we have reached only the corner of one street."

Of course, Attar was not the first Sufi master to make his literary mark; for example, Qushayri (d. 1074) wrote a major handbook, *The Stages of the Path.* Nor was Attar the first to teach by using poetry and storytelling; Sana'i (d. 1131), the author of *The Walled Garden of Truth,* is probably the one who deserves the credit for that. However, compared with Attar, no other poet, not even Rumi, is as straightforward and direct in the art of storytelling. Attar's tales are easy for the layperson to understand. Although they contain hidden symbolic messages for those who are familiar with Sufi principles, the stories also convey simple lessons of morality and humanity. Attar chose subjects and characters with which the common people were familiar, such as Sulayman (Solomon), Ibrahim (Abraham), Yusuf (Joseph), and Isa (Jesus). Even though Attar wrote verse, his humility did not allow him to consider himself a poet—and in fact, he paid no attention to the conventions of poetry in his poems. Nevertheless, some of the world's most impressive poems were penned by this master. Writing about Attar's work, Rumi says, "I am the Master of Rum [the ancient city of Iconium, from which Rumi took his name], whose words are sweet as sugar, yet in speaking I am but a servant to Attar."

Attar was born around 1136 in Nishapur in Persia, less than a century before Genghis Khan's conquest of Asia and a portion of Europe. His pen name, Attar—meaning "chemist" or "perfumer"—alluded to the fact that he operated a pharmacy in his hometown. A wealthy man, he was able to employ more than thirty men in his store. Exactly when Attar started to write Sufi poems is not known; however, researchers agree on one particular incident that drove Attar into a life of inner quest and teaching. There are many versions of the story of this event—a conversation between Attar and a dervish. What follows is the most common version.

One day a dervish who came to Attar's pharmacy to ask for medicine was amazed by the magnificence of the shop. Wide-eyed, he looked about the shop and then began to scrutinize Attar's appearance. Attar asked the man why he was staring at him.

"I was wondering how you are going to die when you have to leave all this wealth behind," the dervish answered.

Feeling insulted, Attar angrily replied, "I will die just as you will."

"But I have nothing to worry about. All I have is the cloak on my back and this *kashkul* [begging bowl]. Now, do you still claim you will die the way I will?"

"Of course," Attar answered.

Upon hearing this, the dervish uttered the name of God and, using his *kashkul* as a pillow, lay down and died.

This incident is supposed to have had such a great impact on Attar that he closed his business and withdrew into a Sufi settlement under the guidance of Ruknuddin, a shaykh of the Kobrawiya Order. Unfortunately, very little is known of Attar's training during this period. What is known is that after a few years he traveled to Mecca on pilgrimage. We might speculate that before this trip he had completed the stages of spiritual development, for after his travels he began to write.

The account of Attar's death is a story in itself. He was killed around 1230 at the hands of one of Genghis Khan's soldiers during the Mongol invasion of Persia. There are many variations of this story; the following is the most common.

One day Attar was captured by a Mongol. As he was being dragged around, someone came along and offered the Mongol a thousand pieces of silver for Attar. Attar advised the Mongol not to accept because the price was not right. The Mongol, heeding the words of Attar, refused to sell him. A while later, another man came by, offering a sack of straw for Attar. Attar told the Mongol, "Sell me now, for this is my price, and that is all I am worth." Upon hearing this, the Mongol became enraged and cut off Attar's head. And so Attar died teaching another lesson in selflessness to the seekers of Truth.

Most of Attar's books have been lost in the course of the centuries. Today, only thirty remain; all are poetry except his *Memoirs of the Saints.* The latter is an important biographical resource that provides information on authors and poets who wrote about the Muslim sages. It starts with an account of Ja'far Sadiq, the Sixth Imam of the Shiites and a great Sufi master of the second century after the Prophet Muhammad (ninth century C.E.), and ends with a biography of Hallaj.[2]

Another work of Attar's, *The Book of God,* is a description of the six faculties of the human being: ego, imagination, intellect, thirst for knowledge, thirst for detachment, and thirst for Unity. Attar likens the human being with these faculties to a king with six sons. Each son comes to the king requesting something, and the king tries to educate his sons about what it is they desire and what implications the fulfillment of their desires would have. The lesson he teaches them is to pursue the Eternal Presence of God as the highest goal. In Attar's words:

> Once the six are tamed and obey the king's orders,
> They will arrive at the Eternal Presence of God.

In his *Book of Secrets,* Attar does not follow his familiar style of "tales within a tale." It is rather just a collection of small stories presented for the sake of elevating the spiritual or moral state of the reader. Rumi used a similar approach in his *Mathnawi,* but the difference between the two works is that whereas Rumi sets the scene to make a point and express his own opinion specifically,

Attar simply presents a tale without offering his own opinion, and thus allows the story to speak for itself.

The Book of Affliction by Attar is based on the story of a traveler who is looking for God. He tries to get roadmaps from imperfect beings who themselves are lost and in need of guidance. In this book, Attar's message is that the world without God is a lonely one, full of suffering, and that the way to God lies within.

The Conference of the Birds is one of the most important works of Sufi literature, by which most if not all Sufi masters have been inspired. It is a collection of fables, jokes, and tales-within-a-tale, all embodied in a single story of spiritual quest, led by the hoopoe bird, which symbolizes the spiritual master. Perhaps no other Sufi master has used such simple language and such easily understood analogies to teach the stages of development on the path toward perfection. We have summarized the main features of the story in our version. (Interested readers are referred to the bibliography for an English version of *The Conference of the Birds,* where the complete work may be found.)

Our stories of Shaykh San'an and Shakir are drawn from the little tales in Attar's *Conference of the Birds*, while the tale of Bahlul comes from *The Book of God*. Bahlul is a particularly notable character who appears in many stories of the Middle East, especially Persia. Whether or not this legendary figure was an actual master is not certain; non-Sufi literature refers to him as a wise man, while Sufi writers, including Attar, clearly portray him as a mystic. What is known about him is that his name was Abu Vahib Ibn Amru and that he was born and raised in Kufa (Iraq) and died around 812 C.E. Because of the unjust social climate created by the caliph of the time, Harun al-Rashid, Bahlul posed as a madman; this guise enabled him to speak and act as he pleased without fear of punishment. The caliph and local rulers were entertained by his antics and allowed him free access to the court. Especially well known are his critical yet humorous remarks about the rulers.

THE CONFERENCE OF THE BIRDS

A group of birds desire to find their king, and so they ask a wise hoopoe (a bird with a fanlike crest) to help them with their quest. The hoopoe tells them that the king they are looking for is called Simurgh (meaning "thirty birds" in Persian) and lives in hiding in the mountain of Kaf—but that it is a difficult and dangerous journey to reach the king. The birds implore the hoopoe to guide them. The hoopoe agrees and starts teaching each bird according to its individual level and temperament. He tells the birds that in order to reach the top of the mountain, they need to traverse five valleys and two deserts; when they have passed the last desert, they will enter the palace of the king.

Those with weak wills, who are afraid of the journey, start making excuses. The parrot, who is egotistical and selfish, says that he will look for the Holy Grail instead of seeking the king. The peacock, the legendary bird of paradise, exclaims that he has dreamed of going back to heaven and will wait patiently for that day. The goose cries that his life depends on being near water, and he will die if he is too far from it. The bittern has a similar excuse; it is not possible for him to travel far from the sea, for his love of water is so great that although he has sat at the shore for years, he has not dared to drink one drop of it, lest the sea run out of water. The night owl declares that he would rather stay and scrounge through ruins in hopes of finding a treasure someday. The nightingale says that he has no need to travel, for he is in love with the rose, and this love is enough for him; he possesses secrets of love that no other creature has. In a wonderful voice, he sings of love:

> I know the secrets of love. All through the night I pour out my love call. The mystical music of the flute is inspired by my lament, and it is I who set the rose to trembling and move the hearts of lovers. I teach mysteries with my sad notes, and whoever hears me is lost in rapture. No one knows my secrets save the rose alone. I

have forgotten myself and think of nothing but the rose. To reach Simurgh—that is beyond me. The love of the rose is enough for the nightingale![3]

The hoopoe, who has been patiently listening, answers the nightingale:

You are preoccupied with the outward shape of things, with the pleasures of a seductive form. Love of the rose has driven thorns into your heart. No matter how great the beauty of the rose, it will vanish in a few days; and love for something so perishable can only cause revulsion in the Perfect One. If the rose smiles at you, it is only to fill you with sorrow, for she laughs at you with each spring. Forsake the rose and her red color.[4]

What is Attar getting at in this simple conversation? We humans have a desire to seek perfection, but many times we tend to stop the process as soon as we detect the slightest sign of progress. This is particularly true for aspirants on the spiritual path: many seekers are enchanted with the early stages of awakening and confuse them with full illumination. Attar warns us of such dangers—we must not mistake love of the imaginary for love of the Real. It is for this reason that the nightingale must give up his deluded attachment to the rose, in order to seek the everlasting Beloved.

The hoopoe regales the other birds with wondrous tales of those who have already made the perilous journey. Attar uses symbolic imagery throughout, and each of the tales, like the story of the nightingale, rewards the reader's contemplation with a deeper understanding.

Having heard the hoopoe's stories, the birds are now inspired to start on their journey and fly toward the first valley. However, as soon as they run into problems, they realize that the path is going to be more difficult than they had imagined. Some start making excuses again. One claims that the hoopoe is not wise enough to lead them. Another complains that Satan has possessed him and is making things difficult for him. Still another expresses his longing for money and the comforts of a luxurious life.

Finally the hoopoe decides that the only way to make the birds understand is to describe to them the seven valleys and deserts of the journey. The first is the Valley of Quest. There one restlessly seeks for the Truth, the hoopoe says. With constancy, one searches for a greater meaning to the purpose of life. Only a dedicated seeker can pass through the first valley safely and fly on to the second, the Valley of Love. Here one feels a limitless desire to see the Beloved King. A burning fire of love starts growing in one's heart and becomes all consuming. This is a more dangerous place than the first valley, because there are obstacles on the way to test one's love. Yet this very same love impels the seeker out of the valley and on to a higher land—the third valley, the Valley of Gnosis. Once one enters this land, one's heart is illuminated with Truth. Here one acquires inner knowledge of the Beloved. Thereafter, the traveler continues the journey into the Valley of Detachment, where he or she loses his desire for earthly possessions. No attachment to the material world exists for the wanderer who traverses this valley; freed of desires, the aspirant is now completely independent.

Each new place the seeker encounters is more dangerous than the previous one, and should be explored step by step, for each holds its own trials and difficulties. Thus, each encounter with a new land is a fresh experience.

The fifth valley is the Valley of Unity. Here the traveler experiences that all beings are one in essence—that all the manifold ideas and experiences and creatures of life have, in actuality, but one Source. The traveler then comes upon the Desert of Astonishment. Now one becomes forgetful of one's own and everyone else's existence. One sees light not with the eye of the mind, but with the eye of the heart. The door to divine treasure, the secret of secrets, is opened. In this land, the ordinary intellect no longer functions.

Here, the traveler who is asked who and what he is, answers, "I know nothing."

Finally comes the Desert of Annihilation and Death. At this point, the aspirant finally understands how a drop merges with the ocean. He is drowned in the Ocean of Unity with the Beloved. He has reached the destination of the journey to find the King.

After hearing the hoopoe's description of what lies ahead, the birds become so excited that they instantly resume their journey. On the way, some die of heat, and some are drowned in the sea; others become tired and cannot continue; one group is hunted by wild animals, and yet others become so distracted by the attractions of the lands through which they are passing that they get lost and are left behind. Only thirty of the birds reach their destination—the Mountain of Kaf.

At the King's palace, the gatekeeper treats the thirty birds unkindly. But the birds, who have already been through the worst, are tolerant and do not allow themselves to be bothered by his harshness. Finally, the King's personal servant comes out and directs the birds to the King's hall. Upon entering, the birds look everywhere, astonished. They do not know what is going on, for instead of seeing Simurgh, "thirty birds," all they see is . . . thirty birds. They finally realize that by looking at themselves, they have found the King, and that in their search for the King, they have found themselves.

Those who pass through the seven cities of Love are purified. When they come to the King's palace, they find the King revealed in the mirror of their hearts.

BAHLUL, A FOOL OF GOD

During the hot summer days in Baghdad, it seems that nothing interesting ever happens to keep the children busy. So the resourceful youngsters respond by inventing their own pastimes, such as annoying vendors in the bazaar by stealing their merchandise—an apple here, a trinket there. How funny it is to picture the poor merchants racing down the narrow alleys of the city after a bunch of laughing kids. At the same time, one has to admit that the impertinent children get just what they deserve once the merchant catches them.

This summer was different, though. The children of Baghdad had found a new plaything to amuse themselves with: "Some kind of strange man," as one of them put it, "who does not look like anyone we know."

Bahlul, the man was called, and he did indeed look extraordinarily different from the rest. Bahlul did not observe the normal etiquette of his time and place. His ragged clothing didn't even resemble that of the town's beggars, consisting as it did of a harsh piece of wool, something like a rice bag—*suf,* the material was called. Its tatters barely covered his emaciated body. His bony structure under the loose bag evoked the image of a skeleton dressed in some kind of ghostly outfit. Yet there was nothing scary about this ghost.

Stranger even than Bahlul's way of dressing was his mysterious face. His dark hair, which looked like it had not been groomed in many years, was long and wild, and his beard, never having been trimmed, came down to his chest. Behind the beard, all one could see was a narrow nose and a pair of eyes. But those eyes—ah, they could tell a whole story in themselves.

In large part, the mystery of Bahlul's character came from those eyes. He had the kind of gaze that one would usually see only in the eyes of a madman. Yet, when one looked carefully, a wisdom could be seen in them, a life of experience and knowledge. They radiated a light of wonder, or perhaps it was love, and there was a mysterious power about that radiating light which made it unbearable for anyone to look into Bahlul's eyes.

The man would wander around all day in alleyways, mumbling

to himself as if talking to some unseen presence, sometimes nodding his head in apparent agreement, at other times smiling or even laughing loudly. So preoccupied was he with this invisible friend that most of the time he would not even notice the intrusion of people who out of curiosity would ask him questions.

The children could not make up their minds about him. At first, they would play their own mean games with him, throwing stones at him or ridiculing his appearance. In response, Bahlul, who usually had his head down and his eyes closed, would slowly lift his head, open his eyes, and smile kindly at them. This response was so unexpected and odd that at first the children weren't sure how to react. Later, however, they heard a rumor that Bahlul was insane. This helped them make up their minds about the strange man.

The rumor originated with a traveling merchant named Ahmad. Ahmad had traveled all around the East, from Persia to China and back, marketing Persian rugs one way and Chinese silk the other. While talking to a friend one day in the bazaar in Baghdad, he happened to come upon the playful crowd of children who had just finished taunting Bahlul.

"You must have a lot of problems with such a nasty bunch of brats, eh?" Ahmad asked his friend.

"We used to," replied the friend, who was named 'Ali, "but thanks to Bahlul, who has become a new hobby for the kids, we can now get on with business here."

"Bahlul, did you say?" asked Ahmad. "So . . . he is here," he continued, without waiting for an answer. "Strange fellow," he murmured thoughtfully.

"You know him?" countered 'Ali. "How could you possibly know such a vagrant and madman?"

And so Ahmad began to tell his friend what he knew about Bahlul. "A strange fellow, for sure. Bahlul has quite a reputation in the eastern lands where I travel. They say he is madly in love with God." Here, Ahmad paused and stared at his companion. "I can see surprise in your face, my friend. I know you think that we all love the Almighty. But from what I have seen and heard about Bahlul, his kind of love is different indeed. Far different. He converses with his Beloved day and night. It is as if he is in love with the most astonishingly beautiful woman in the universe. She has stolen his heart and soul totally. He carries her with himself everywhere, talking to her all his waking and even sleeping moments."

The traveling merchant paused to catch his breath, and then went on. "One day Bahlul's love for the Almighty got so out of hand that he left his home, quit his job, and started wandering— only God Himself knows with what purpose. Since that time, he has become so totally lost in love that he has abandoned all thought of anything but God, ignoring his own appearance and well-being. This man has no time for himself, and that's why his clothes are so ragged and his hair and beard have grown so long. 'Any moment that is not spent paying attention to the Beloved,' Bahlul has said, 'is a moment wasted.'"

A silence fell between the two men. Ahmad stood staring off into space, while his companion gazed at him in disbelief. "What kind of story is this?" 'Ali asked himself. He found it hard to believe that anyone would turn his back on the world and everything in it solely for the love of God. "What does this Bahlul hope to achieve?" he wondered.

It was as if Ahmad had heard this friend's unspoken question, for at that moment he began to speak again. "Some could not understand Bahlul. They wondered about the meaning of such a mad love. They could not comprehend that all the lover wants is to be with the Beloved: to see her, praise her, worship her, become annihilated in her. Oneness with the Beloved is the lover's only aim. It is not that unreasonable when you think about it. If you were madly in love with a woman, would you not wish to spend all your life with her? Would you not want to be with her always?"

Without waiting for an answer again, Ahmad went on. "It is the same way with the one who falls in love with God, or so I have been told. For some reason, I believe that Bahlul has already been united with his Beloved. Can't you see it in his eyes? Don't you see that such a fire burns in his eyes that it could set one ablaze from looking at it? The wisdom hidden within him, his utmost kindness toward all creatures, his smiling face even when people make fun of him and abuse him — all these have to come from God Himself, for no human being can attain such heights on his or her own." As if drained by his speech, Ahmad fell silent. His friend, ashamed of having asked his question, looked down and kept busy kicking the pebbles underneath his cart.

"It is an amazing story that you have told, brother," 'Ali said finally, breaking the silence. "I can see now that this man's behavior does in fact make a strange kind of sense. But don't expect everybody to understand him."

Ahmad nodded. "This has always been the problem wherever Bahlul has gone. He has always been treated like a madman just because he is not understood."

For hours the two friends went on speaking of Bahlul and his love. The more they spoke, the more their hearts desired to hear about love. And the more they talked of love, the more their souls yearned to see the Truth.

Just as 'Ali had intimated, few understood Bahlul. His reputation as a madman brought him a great deal of hardship. No one would sell him anything; no one was willing to talk to him or answer his questions, though he asked them in the most kindly manner. Eventually, people decided that Bahlul was possessed by the devil himself. The children, of course, made sure that they gave this "evil" character what he deserved. They swore at him, threw things at him, and even beat him with sticks, all in the misguided expectation that Bahlul would finally complain and beg for mercy. But, much to their dismay, the man would not show the slightest sign of discomfort or anger. He would simply continue with his prayers and smile at the children, bestowing blessings upon them. "How," he would sometimes say, "can one who is content with God ever complain of anything?"

For Bahlul, all that came to him came from God. Therefore, he accepted with happiness all the verbal and physical abuse heaped upon him as a gift from his Beloved. After one particularly bad beating by a gang of teenagers, though, Bahlul decided to leave for Basra, a nearby city that had a reputation for hospitality.

The journey was a difficult one because Bahlul was in such bad shape from the beating he had gotten. His body was sore all over, and his legs ached. He would limp some distance and then have to rest to gather his strength. Yet not once did he stop smiling and talking to his Beloved. The summer had brought such a hot day that it was unbearable to stand in the sun, yet even this did not seem to bother him.

It was past midnight when Bahlul finally arrived at the gates of the city. They were closed, however, since regulations required them to be bolted each day at dusk. Bahlul was hungry, thirsty, and tired. While wandering around trying to decide what he should do next, he happened to notice a man wrapped in a blanket, lying by one of the city walls. "I can rest by this man and have his body's protection from the night's cold breeze," thought Bahlul. So he lay down next to the man and went to sleep, content with what God had provided.

At dawn, just as Bahlul had closed his eyes after morning prayers, he felt a sharp object poke him in the shoulder. He opened his eyes to the daylight, only to find himself surrounded by a group of soldiers. Although half asleep, he began to realize that the body next to him was covered with blood. Bahlul had, in fact, been sleeping beside a corpse, apparently that of someone who had been murdered, though the dark night had kept him unaware of that fact. Looking down, he saw that his own clothing was also soaked with blood, undoubtedly from the murder victim.

"Do you know anyone in this city who can testify to your character?" the head soldier demanded.

"I have only one Friend in the whole world, and that is God," Bahlul exclaimed. At this, the soldiers all began to laugh.

As you might expect, Bahlul was taken to jail, for his claim of innocence appeared absurd and totally implausible. Besides, he looked crazy enough to have committed a murder. The jailer quickly came to the conclusion that Bahlul was guilty and that his lying down by the corpse was a devious attempt to give the impression that he had not committed the act. The jailer sent a report to the hakim, or governor, of the city, who also held the position of the town's supreme judge, and asked him for a ruling on the case.

The hakim's decision came with great speed. Bahlul was found guilty and was to be hanged in public as a lesson to society. The execution was to take place as soon as possible.

It was noon of the same day when Bahlul found out about his fate. Facing inside his cell, he blamed himself for not having been patient enough to endure the pain inflicted upon by the people of Baghdad. "Surrender," he told himself. "Are you just idly claiming that you love Him? If you really love God, you should trust Him completely. For God is absolute Goodness, and all He does is for the best. So be it then, whatever happens."

By the next morning, a crowd had gathered in the central square of the city to get the best positions for viewing this eventful punishment. The execution platform, which had been built the night before, stood ready for its victim. It was a quiet, still morning. In the distance one could hear the sound of the blacksmith's hammer pounding on hot iron. On one corner of the square stood a grocer arranging apples and grapes on his cart for sale later in the morning. Life was going on normally; no one seemed to be the slightest bit saddened by the dark fate that awaited Bahlul.

It was just before sunrise when the execution crew brought Bahlul to the square. The jailer began to give a speech, noting, of course, that crime does not pay and that wrongdoers always get their just punishment at the hands of God's representatives on earth. Then he went on to praise the current caliph, Harun al-Rashid, the prince of all Muslims, and, in turn, his representative, the Hakim of Basra. Thereafter, he gave a signal to the executioner to start the proceedings.

As the command of execution came from the jailer, Bahlul spoke up and asked if he could be granted a last request—a prayer for his soul. The jailer agreed, and an eerie silence fell upon the square. The sun had just begun to rise, and, with its rays falling upon him, Bahlul seemed perfectly calm. Raising his head toward the sun, he stared at the horizon and whispered something slowly. Then he looked out at the crowd, smiled at them, and, without even acknowledging the jailer, made a gesture to the executioner, signaling that he was ready.

The executioner wrapped the noose around Bahlul's thin neck. Seconds after he had pulled the rope tight, a loud scream interrupted the proceedings. "Stop! Please, for the sake of the Almighty, don't do it!" The crowd parted and a man, clearly distraught, approached the stage. "You are making a terrible mistake. This man is innocent," he cried.

The jailer lifted his hand to stop the executioner and ordered the guards to bring the man forward. At the sight of the jailer, the man fell to his knees and confessed: "I am the one you are looking for. I am the murderer, not this wretched man." He refused to say anything further except in the presence of the hakim. This was just as well, for the jailer had no idea what to do next.

Bahlul and the newcomer were both taken to the hakim. Bowing to him, the jailer recounted the whole story briefly, asking for his decision. The hakim, who was considered a fair and just ruler, questioned the two accused men about the truth of the event. Bahlul remained silent, but the other man spoke freely: "I am a butcher, your honor. Until two days ago, I lived with honesty and tried to help people in whatever way I could. Then a friend of mine visited me at my small shop, down the alley from the city square. Before I knew it, we had gotten into an argument. Because of a certain comment he made about me, I flew into a rage and attacked him with the knife that I had been using to cut meat. When I finally calmed down, I saw that I had cut his throat. I was panic-stricken at what I had done and at the thought of what was going to happen to me. Without even being aware of what I was doing, I wrapped him in a blanket and took his body out through the city gates and placed it by one of the walls."

As the man fell silent, the hakim went into deep thought. He looked majestic in his blue and gold robe, gold turban, and matching sandals. As he played with his thick, dark beard, he moved his heavy weight on the big day bed, on which he leaned against many colorful satin pillows. After a few minutes, he glanced up from the tapestry of his expensive Persian rug and asked, "What made you change your mind and confess to your crime?"

"Fear, your majesty. When the executioner started to pull the rope around this man's neck, I suddenly had a vision. I was falling into a dragon's mouth. It was a misery a thousand times worse than being hanged and going to hell itself, for the beast told me that if I didn't speak up at that very moment, he was going to take me with him. I could feel the heat coming from his mouth and see his ugly, rotting teeth, dripping saliva like a volcano's boiling lava."

When the man had finished, the hakim glanced over at Bahlul and nodded at him. "If this man is the murderer, then who are you, and what is your role in all this? Where do you come from, and how did you happen to be beside the victim's body that night?"

"My name is Bahlul. I am a traveler and have no specific occupation. I do whatever God determines for me to do to get by and earn the bread I eat." Then he told how he had come to sleep beside the corpse.

Upon hearing Bahlul's account, the hakim stood and said, "My judgment is that this butcher must be hanged as soon as possible for the murder he committed. As for Bahlul, being entirely blameless, he is welcome to stay in my court for as long as he desires, as a compensation for the difficult times he has had to endure through no fault of his own.

"But your honor," Bahlul interrupted, "the Almighty is nothing but Love. He loves those who forgive and those who love others. He is the Kindest of the Kind, and loves those who treat His creation with loving-kindness. Therefore, it would be a divine act for you to set this man free and forgive him of his guilt. For he has already confessed, and regrets his crime."

The judge remained silent for a moment and then spoke: "My friend, is it not true that the Almighty has appointed us His representatives here on earth to prevent harm from coming to others and to carry out His will?"

"This is true, but perhaps we do not always know exactly what that will is. He alone knows all hearts and can discern the guilty and the innocent. To God, one who is in our eyes a murderer may be innocent and dear, and a righteous person may be a wrongdoer. God is the most knowledgeable."

The hakim could not hide a smile of admiration. "I feel speechless before your words. Since killing this man would not bring back the murdered one, and since he has come forward and admitted his guilt with remorse, I give my consent to his freedom, under the condition that the family of the victim agree upon a sum of money that this man must pay as compensation according to the law."

When all was done and the hakim and Bahlul were finally alone, the two of them took a walk in the hakim's garden. They were quiet for a long time. Then the hakim broke the silence by asking a question that had been bothering him for quite a while: "If you can trust me, then tell me something, my friend. I have heard that you were exceedingly calm at the time of the execution. What gave you such assurance that you were not going to be killed?"

"My calmness," Bahlul replied, gazing directly into the hakim's eyes, "was not due to the assurance that I would not be hanged. Rather, I was sure that the outcome would be whatever the Almighty determined was for the best, and that it had to be. Thus, I surrendered to His will with total contentment. This, in turn, was what brought peace to me, creating such tranquillity and calmness."

Although he had gotten his answer, the hakim was still intrigued by this strange man and wanted to know more. "Tell me, my friend, what was your last prayer before the rope was wrapped around your neck? I am told that no one could make it out."

"I was not praying in the sense that you mean it, for one who trusts in God knows that the Creator of all things knows well what He is doing. It is not for us to ask Him to alter the course of events that He has ordained. For a lover of God, whatever happens is best." Here, Bahlul paused for a second, stroked his beard, and then went on. "Actually, what I was doing was talking to my Lord. I told Him that He knew quite well that I loved Him and that nothing He did would change my love for Him, unless He so willed it. If He chose to send me bitter poison, I would nevertheless take it as sweet sugar and a cherished gift."

Bahlul seemed momentarily to forget where he was, for he suddenly began to address God as if he were back on the scaffold: "O Lord, I am innocent and about to die for a crime that I have not committed. Yet I am not sad, angry, or bitter with You. You know who the killer and the killed are. You also know why things have happened the way they have. It was You who directed me to leave

Baghdad and come to this city, I now realize. It was You alone Who led me to sleep beside the corpse. It was You Who left me there for the soldiers to discover. Therefore, do what You will with me, since You and only You are behind all this."

Bahlul stopped abruptly at this point, as if awakening from a dream. Remembering where he was, he politely apologized to the hakim. The hakim, who was fascinated by Bahlul's state, brushed aside the apology and asked impatiently, "But are you not bitter at all? Do you not want an explanation for all that has happened?"

Bahlul started laughing upon hearing this, and went on for a long time. "Dear hakim," he finally managed to say, stifling his mirth, "God is Lord. He does whatever He pleases, for whatever reason He sees fit. Who are we to question His actions or express an opinion about His decisions? It is enough for me to love Him. I need no explanations."

THIS TOO SHALL PASS

A dervish who had traveled long and hard through the desert finally came to civilization after a long journey. The village was called Sandy Hills, and it was dry and hot. Except for the hay feed and some shrubs, not much greenery was to be found. Cattle were the main means of livelihood for the people of Sandy Hills; had the condition of the soil been different, they might have been able to engage in agriculture as well. The dervish politely asked a passerby if there was someplace where he could find food and lodging for the night. "Well," said the man, scratching his head, "we don't have such a place in our village, but I am sure Shakir would be happy to provide for you tonight." Then the man gave directions to the ranch owned by Shakir, whose name means "one who thanks the Lord constantly."

On his way to the ranch, the dervish stopped by a small group of old men who were smoking pipes, to reconfirm his directions.

From them, he found out that Shakir was the richest man in the area. One of the men said Shakir owned more than a thousand cattle— "And this is more than the wealth of Haddad, who lives in the neighboring village."

A short while later, the dervish was standing in front of Shakir's home, admiring it. As it turned out, Shakir was a very hospitable and kind person. He insisted that the dervish stay a couple of days in his house. Shakir's wife and daughters were just as kind and considerate as he was and provided the dervish with the best. At the end of his stay, they even supplied him with plenty of food and water for his journey.

On his way back into the desert, the dervish could not help puzzling over the meaning of Shakir's last words at the time of farewell. The dervish had said, "Thank God that you are well off."

"But, dervish," Shakir had replied, "don't be fooled by appearances, for this too shall pass."

During his years on the Sufi path the dervish had come to understand that anything he heard or saw during his journey offered a lesson to be learned and thus was worthy of contemplation. In fact, that was the reason he had undertaken the journey in the first place—to learn more. The words of Shakir occupied his thoughts, and he was not sure if he fully understood their import.

As he sat under the shade of a single tree to pray and meditate, he recalled from his Sufi training that if he kept silent and did not rush to any conclusions, he would eventually find the answer. For he had been taught to be silent and not ask questions; when it was time for him to be enlightened, he would be. Therefore, he shut the door on his thoughts and drowned his soul in a deep meditative state.

And so he passed five more years of traveling to different lands, meeting new people, and learning from his experiences along the way. Every adventure offered a new lesson to be learned. Meanwhile, as Sufi custom required, he remained quiet, concentrating on the instructions of his heart.

One day, the dervish found himself returning to Sandy Hills, the same village at which he had stopped a few years before. He remembered his friend Shakir and asked after him. "He lives in the neighboring village, ten miles from here. He now works for Haddad," a villager answered. The surprised dervish remembered that Haddad was another wealthy man in the region. Happy at the prospect of seeing Shakir again, he rushed toward the neighboring village.

At Haddad's marvelous home, the dervish was welcomed by Shakir, who looked much older now and was dressed in rags. "What happened to you?" the dervish wanted to know. Shakir replied that a flood three years previously had left him with no cattle and no house. So he and his family had become servants of Haddad, who had survived the flood and now enjoyed the status of wealthiest man in that area. This turn of fortune, however, had not changed the kind and friendly manner of Shakir and his family. They graciously took care of the dervish in their cottage for a couple of days, and gave him food and water before he left.

As he was leaving, the dervish said, "I am so sorry for what has happened to you and your family. I know that God has a reason for what He does."

"Oh, but remember, this too shall pass."

Shakir's voice kept echoing in the dervish's ears. The man's smiling face and calm spirit never left his mind. "What in the world does he mean by that statement this time?" The dervish now knew that Shakir's final words on his previous visit had anticipated the changes that had occurred. But this time, he wondered what could justify such an optimistic remark. So, again, he let it pass, preferring to wait for the answer.

Months and years passed, and the dervish, who was getting on in years, kept on traveling without any thought of retiring.

Strangely enough, the pattern of his journeys always brought him back to the village where Shakir lived. This time it took seven years before he got back to Sandy Hills, and by this time Shakir had become rich again. He now lived in the main building of Haddad's compound instead of in the small cottage. "Haddad died a couple of years ago," Shakir explained, "and since he had no heir, he decided to leave me his wealth as a reward for my loyal services.

As the visit drew to a close, the dervish prepared for his greatest journey: he would cross Saudi Arabia for the pilgrimage to Mecca on foot, a long-standing tradition among his colleagues. His farewell with his old friend was no different from the others. Shakir repeated his favorite saying, "This too shall pass."

After the pilgrimage, the dervish traveled to India. Upon returning to his motherland, Persia, he decided to visit Shakir one more time to find out what had become of him. So once again he set out for the village of Sandy Hills. But instead of finding his friend Shakir there, he was shown a modest grave with the inscription, "This too shall pass." He was more surprised at this than he had been on any of the occasions when Shakir himself had spoken those words. "Riches come and riches go," thought the dervish to himself, "but how can a tomb change?"

From that time on, the dervish made it a point to visit the tomb of his friend every year, when he would spend a few hours meditating at Shakir's abode. However, on one of his visits, he found the cemetery and the grave gone, washed away by a flood. Now the old dervish had lost the only traces left of a man who had marked the experiences of his life so exceptionally. The dervish stayed at the ruins of the cemetery for hours, staring at the ground. Finally, he lifted his head to the sky and then, as if discovering a greater meaning, nodded his head as a sign of confirmation and said, "This too shall pass."

When the dervish had finally become too old to travel, he decided to settle down and live the rest of his life in peace and quiet.

Years passed by, and the old man spent his time helping those who came to him for advice and sharing his experiences with the young. People came from all over to have the benefit of his wisdom. Eventually his fame spread to the king's great advisor, who happened to be looking for someone with great wisdom.

The fact was, the king desired a ring be made for him. The ring was to be a special one: it was to carry an inscription such that if the king was sad, he could look at the ring and it would make him happy, and if he was happy, he could look at the ring and it would make him sad.

The best jewelers were hired, and many men and women came forward with suggestions for the ring, but the king liked none of them. So the advisor wrote to the dervish explaining the situation, asking for help, and inviting him to the palace. Without leaving home, the dervish sent back his reply.

A few days later, an emerald ring was made and presented to the king. The king, who had been depressed for days, reluctantly put the ring on his finger and glanced at it with a disappointed sigh. Then he started to smile, and a few moments later, he was laughing loudly. One the ring were inscribed the words, "This too shall pass."

SHAYKH SAN'AN

A long time ago, in the land of Arabia, in the city of Mecca, there lived a pious Sufi shaykh, a great teacher, named San'an. For fifty years he had devoted his life to serving God and His creatures. Living in a sanctuary, the shaykh guided aspirants on their spiritual journey, and at night, in his humble prayer, he shared mysteries of creation with his Beloved Lord. Those who came to Mecca on pilgrimage also came to visit the shaykh—to hear his advice and to learn from his teachings. He had four hundred disciples, all faithful to him, all prepared to obey his instructions regardless of their own will and desire. They believed in their teacher whole-heartedly, having left their families and homes out of devotion to him.

One night, San'an had a dream. He saw himself in the city of Rum in the empire of Byzantium, bowing to an idol. The shaykh awoke in distress, fearing that this dream might be a warning from his Lord about a future event. He tried to dismiss it, telling himself that it was only a dream and it had no significance. But to his dismay, he had the same dream over and over in the nights to come. When he could no longer ignore this haunting nightmare, he decided to set out for Byzantium to find out what his Lord had in store for him.

As San'an was preparing to leave, many of his disciples insisted on accompanying him, as the custom of the time prescribed. San'an warned them that the journey might be unpleasant, but the students were persistent. So San'an and his disciples set out, walking day and night, rain or shine, and no one complained of hardship even once.

Finally they arrived at the outskirts of Rum, near a temple. As they were wandering about the place, the shaykh heard a soul-touching voice, softer than a breeze, lighter than a feather, singing a love song that would make any heart bleed with desire. As the shaykh followed the voice, he noticed an open window on the second floor of the temple. A young Christian woman was sitting at the window combing her long, golden hair and singing a sad song. The reflection of the light on her hair, her rosy, glossy lips slightly parted as if ready for a kiss, and her marble-white neck showing through the open collar of her dress created a vision so powerful that even a pious man like San'an became absorbed in gazing upon it. As if glued to the spot, the shaykh could not budge. His heart was beating fast, and he felt he could barely breathe. In a moment shorter than a sigh, the old man had lost his heart to the Christian girl. Finally he sat down where he was, shivering all over and crying, "O dear Lord! What has become of me? What fire is this, burning my soul, robbing me of my existence?"

San'an sat in the consuming fire of a love that was taking over his mind and soul. In a moment, he had forgotten who he was and where he had come from. Nothing mattered to him anymore except seeing the young woman's face again. Yet she did not stay long; she left the window and disappeared without even noticing the wails and cries of the shaykh.

The disciples, finding their teacher in such agony, wondering helplessly what to do. Thinking that the shaykh might be simply passing through a stage, they tried to suggest this possibility to him, but to no avail. The shaykh did not hear what they were saying and just stood staring at the now-empty window of the girl's room.

Night was approaching, and the shaykh became even more distressed as he realized he would have to wait until morning to see his love again. It seemed that the dark of night brought him a strong love potion, which intensified his longing, and his heart bled more profusely. He wailed and crawled in the dirt. He clawed at the soil and squeezed it into his shaking hands, soaking it with his tears. "Never has the night seemed so endless," he cried. "Nights of agony I have had before, yet none resembling this one, none causing me so much pain, none being so long as this one. I feel like a candle that won't last the night. My light will be extinguished by sunrise, and I will not survive to tell the story of this dreadful night. No longer have I any patience to lead me through the dark — neither have I a mind to convince me with reason of the morning's coming. My body is crushed under the heavy burden of this love. Where are my hands that I might at least bury myself under the dirt so that I will not have to endure such separation, or my legs that I might take myself to my love! If only I had a friend whose sympathy would relieve me! Oh, to think that I have nothing left anymore. I have given all away in this plundering love!"

The students gathered around their distressed shaykh and cried

with him all night, not because they understood, but rather in
sorrow and confusion about what had happened to their teacher.

So it was that San'an fell madly in love with a Christian girl who
served in the temple. Such madness came over him that he forgot
all about his past. It was as if he knew the world no more; all that
mattered for him was a pair of enchanting blue eyes that seemed
to follow him around wherever he went.

On the second night, San'an became exceedingly restless. His
students again gathered around him, worried about his state. They
thought they might yet be able to talk him out of his obsession.
Each one went to him with advice or a suggestion.

"Why don't you forget about the girl? Perform the ablution for
cleansing your soul, and then we can all go home."

"My ablution has already been done with the blood of my injured heart. Don't talk to me of ablution, you who know nothing
of love's bleeding heart!"

"If you repent of your sin, God will forgive you, for you have
been a shaykh for many years."

"What I have repented of is my shaykhhood and no more."

"You are our guide to the Light, the one who knows the way to
God. If you pray to Him, surely He will hear and forgive you."

"I pray for her, for she is the focus of all my prayers."

"Are you not regretful of this love that has driven you totally
out of reason?"

"I am indeed regretful, but only of one thing—that I did not
fall in love sooner."

"Don't you care what others think? What will people say when
they hear that their pious shaykh has gone astray?"

"What people say about me does not matter to me anymore.
Why should I care what label they attach to me? I am free from
that now."

"Don't you care anything about your friends of a lifetime—

about us and your other disciples? Don't you realize that it breaks
our hearts to see you this way?"

"All I care about is to see my beloved happy. No one else exists
for me anymore."

"Come on, let's all go back to Mecca and its Ka'ba and forget
about this journey and what happened here."

"My only Mecca is this temple, and its Ka'ba is the girl. It is in
this place that one can get drunk of love and not there."

"At least be mindful of paradise. You are old and do not have
much time left. If you have any hope of heaven, give up this sense-
lessness."

"What heaven could be more beautiful than the angelic face of
my beloved? What do I need that paradise for, when I have this
one?"

"Have you no shame before God Almighty? For years, He has
been your sole occupation. How can you betray Him now?"

"How can I escape this trap that God Himself has set for me?"

"O good shaykh, this is our last request to you. For God's sake,
come back to the faith and do not abandon us, your students."

"Do not make such a request of me. I am drowned in blasphemy, and for one who abandons faith and chooses blasphemy,
there is no return."

When the disciples found their reasoning useless, they decided
to retire to a place nearby where they could be close to San'an in
case he should change his mind. The only way they could endure
the pain of losing their master was by nourishing the hope that
soon everything could be back to normal again.

Days and nights passed, yet no change took place. San'an settled
down in a spot across from the temple, where stray dogs usually
gathered, and made it his home. It was located alongside the path
the young woman took to town. Hoping she would notice him, the
shaykh sat there patiently, gazing at her with longing as she passed

by. Yet she never even glanced his way and always continued on her way toward the city as if she had not noticed him at all.

Not even knowing his beloved's name, the shaykh had given her a name of his own—Sunshine. He composed poetry in her name, singing the verses in sad melodies. He was consumed so much by his love that he no longer cared about eating or sleeping. If anyone happened to toss some scraps to the stray dogs, he would have a share of the food; otherwise he went hungry without even noticing it.

Finally, the young woman noticed the strange old man sitting in the dust. Overcome by curiosity, she asked, "Why do you reside here with the dogs? Don't you have a home or relatives to go to?"

Overjoyed by the girl's attention, the shaykh replied, "I know no home, no relatives. All I know is that I have fallen in love with you, and will stay here until you find me worthy of your love."

Sunshine laughed at the shaykh's reply and mocked him with her disgust. "Are you not ashamed of yourself? You are old enough to be my grandfather. A man of your age is only worthy of the grave. A girl as young and beautiful as I am deserves a handsome young man."

"Love knows no age. No matter how young or old a person is, love affects him just the same. I am your devotee, and will do whatever you say."

So eloquently did the master speak of his love and his pain that gradually the young woman became convinced of his sincerity. Indeed, she realized, he would do anything she desired. And so she addressed San'an thus: "If what you claim is true, then you must renounce your faith and convert to ours. You must burn your Holy Book and abandon any obligations your religion requires. You must drink wine and cast off your mantle of shaykhhood."

San'an replied calmly to this startling demand: "Love sets many challenges for a lover. Its tests are bloody and cruel, yet the result is sweet and comforting. The true lover knows no faith, for love itself is his belief. He knows no status, for there is no position higher than that of love."

When the Byzantine monks and clerics heard that a great Sufi master had agreed to abandon his faith, they celebrated. They arranged a ritual in which the shaykh threw the Qur'an into the fire. He tore off his robe and put on the Christian cincture. Then he drank wine and bowed to the girl in submission. He rejoiced with the others, singing, "I have become nothing for love. I have become disgraced in love. No one has seen what I can see with the eyes of love."

While the Christians were celebrating, the shaykh's disciples were lamenting. As shattered and heartbroken as they were, it seemed that their master did not see their agony or hear their wailing.

San'an had worshipfully obeyed the command of his beloved — no matter that it violated all that he stood for. And yet even this was not enough: he still longed to prove his love by fulfilling her every whim. And so he asked, "What more can I do for you?"

The young woman put her head back and laughed. "You must spend money on me. I want jewels, gold, and coins of silver. If you don't have it, don't waste your time, old man, and get out of my sight."

The shaykh responded that he had nowhere to go but the temple, for he had lost his own being in hers. That he possessed nothing but a heart, and it had already been given away to her. That he could not live without her—he had not the fortitude for separation. He would do anything she desired of him, if only he could live in union with her.

"My marriage terms," she said thoughtfully, "are that you tend my pigs for a year. Once the year has passed and you have completed the job satisfactorily, I will be ready to become your wife."

San'an gladly took up residence in the pigsty and with loving attention took care of those animals so loathed by the Muslims.

The sight of their teacher living among the pigs was too embar-
rassing for the students. They came to the shaykh and pleaded with
him. "What should we do now? Do you want us to convert as
well? We will stay with you if you tell us to do so."

San'an told them that he wanted nothing from them and that
they should go their own way. If anyone asked them about him,
they should tell the truth. Now they should leave and let him take
care of the pigs, for he had no time to waste on them.

Crying all the way, the disciples went back to Mecca. When
they arrived, they secluded themselves out of fear of having to
explain to others what had happened in Rum. Yet there was one
person they could not avoid. This was a fellow student who had
been on a journey when the shaykh and his pupils had left for
Rum. When he came back home and could not find his master, he
asked the others about him. The disciples then had to tell him the
entire story.

When they finished, he cried from the depth of his heart and
shouted at them in anger. "What kind of disciples are you? If you
claim to love our master, you must be true to your claim. You
should be ashamed of yourselves! If your master threw off his Sufi
cloak and put on a cincture, you should have done the same. If he
lived in a pigsty, you should have followed him. That is what love
demands—no matter that it be labeled scandalous or insane. How
did you dare to judge our shaykh as having done wrong? What gave
you the authority to advise him to abandon his love?"

Thus shamed by their companion, the disciples lowered their
heads sorrowfully. In remorse, they entered into a long retreat at
the loyal disciple's house, during which they neither ate nor drank.

On the fortieth day, the loyal disciple, who had been crying day
and night in selfless grief for his master, had a vision. A cloud of
dark dust from the temple hovered between the shaykh and God.
Suddenly the dust arose from the path, and the shaykh was embraced by the Light. Then a voice of eternity declared: "One must

be burned in the fire of Love to be worthy of seeing the Eternal Beloved. Name and position have no value in the creed of Love. Before one can behold the Truth, the dust of existence must be cleansed from the mirror of the soul. Only then can one see the reflection of the True Beloved in the mirror."

The disciple ran to his friends and told them of his vision. Wasting no time, they all made their way back to Rum.

Outside the city they found the shaykh with his forehead on the ground in servitude to God. Having passed beyond mosque and temple, liberated from both Islam and Christianity, having lost all attachment to status or piety, he was free from self, united with his True Beloved. The shaykh was silent, yet his eyes shone with the secret joy known only to the Beloved and the lover. The disciples gathered around their master. The shaykh joined his students again. Together they set out for Mecca.

In the meantime, the young woman whom San'an had named Sunshine had a powerful dream. In it the Lord appeared to her as the sun. She fell to the ground, crying, "Oh, dear Lord, how ignorant is the one who has not seen You! How lost I have been who have not known You. Show me the path to You, for now that I have seen Your beauty, I can live no more without You. Nor shall I rest a moment until I unite with You."

The young woman fell into a trance and wept for hours. At last a call came from the heavens: "Go to the shaykh. He is the one to show you the way."

She rushed outside without even putting on her shoes. When she found out that San'an had left for Mecca, she ran outside the city and into the desert in search of the master's caravan. But it was too late; the caravan had left hours before. The barefoot girl ran for days and nights with neither food nor water. All along the way, her tears moistened the dry sand. She cried out in pain and distress, calling to her master with love and devotion.

Her cries reached the heart of the shaykh. Inwardly he understood that the young woman had left all she had in order to search for her Beloved. San'an informed his disciples of the news and sent them searching for her. They found the pitiful figure collapsed in the sand from thirst and exhaustion, calling for her shaykh.

In the presence of the master, the young woman threw herself at his feet, beseeching him: "Great master, I am burning with love. I long to see my Beloved. Yet my eyes see nothing but darkness. Help me see Him, for I can wait no more without my Lord." The shaykh took her hands gently and gazed into her eyes as if looking into her soul, guiding her spirit to God through his own. The young woman screamed, "O Love, I can bear separation no more. Farewell, great master of all ages!" So saying, Sunshine abandoned her soul to her Beloved and died.

San'an stood motionless for a time. The disciples feared that he had gone mad again. However, the master eventually lifted his head and stared far into the desert as he spoke: "Fortunate are those who complete the journey and unite with the Beloved. Free are they, for in union with God they live."

And then he sighed and added, "And sad is the lot of those whose destiny is to guide others to the Goal—for they must abandon the precious state of union and be bound for the sake of His pleasure and will!"

HAKIM NIZAMI

Narrator of Love Stories

PERSIA'S leading medieval epic poet, Hakim Nizami of Ganje, is especially renowned for two romantic tales: *Layla and Majnun,* and *Khusrau and Shirin.* The sad story of Majnun (literally, "love-crazed"), whose love for the unattainable Layla drives him mad, has been recited for centuries by bards from city to city, and has inspired countless Persian miniaturists, who enjoyed depicting Majnun in the wilderness, surrounded by the wild animals who were attracted to him. Equally dramatic is the tale of the Armenian princess Shirin (pronounced *Shireen*), who falls in love with a Persian king named Khusrau; the hands of fate keep the two apart so that the king might learn the true meaning of love. The agony of thwarted love and the death of the lovers at the end have made both these stories particularly poignant for their listeners.

As these stories spread, people began to learn about the writer himself. It was said that Nizami was a Sufi master and that the beloved in his stories was, in truth, God. Through these stories people learned that a spiritual seeker's quest for union with the Beloved is an endeavor that leads to the annihilation of the limited identity of the lover in the infinite being of the Beloved.

The details of Nizami's life story are not very clear. In the introductory verses of *Layla and Majnun* he points out that he was given the name Ilyas (Elijah) at birth and that Nizami was his nickname.

Some historians have indicated 1155 as his date of birth, while others have reported years as late as 1162. His birthplace was the city of Ganje, a short distance from today's Bakou in the former Soviet Azerbaijan in northwestern Iran. But Nizami's mother was of the Kurdish tribe, and his father's ancestors were from Iraq, so it is not surprising that the settings for his two famous works are the Arabian desert and the Kurdish mountains of western Iran.

Nizami died in 1222 or 1223 and was buried in Ganje. Apparently a shrine was built for him there that eventually fell into ruin. Recently the government of Azerbaijan rebuilt the tomb and repaired its damaged courtyard.

Nizami was well versed in all the sciences of his time, such as mathematics, Islamic canon law, Greek philosophy, and medicine. Early in life he embarked on the mystic's path, but no more is known of his training. Nizami himself suggests that he had reached some very high levels of spirituality, since he alludes to the fact that he was taught by Khidr, the mysterious guide who appears to pilgrims on the path, and that he enjoyed the protection of the ninety-nine Most Beautiful Names of God.

Six major works by Nizami—including *Layla and Majnun* and *Khusrau and Shirin*—were composed in the poetical style known as *mathnawi*, consisting of rhymed couplets. (This form was perfected by Rumi, one of whose famous books is titled the *Mathnawi*.) Although these works take the form of stories, they contain many hidden lessons for spiritual seekers. The level of the teachings varies from those intended for the general public to those designed for initiates of a Sufi order. Nizami's writing is noted for its refined language and its ingenious puns, so difficult to reproduce in translation.

In *The Source of Secrets*, Nizami told stories that had not been told before. In fact, even the style of poetry was new, original to him. He composed this work of about 2,260 lines when he was about thirty years old.

Khusrau and Shirin is about 6,500 lines in length. We offer a prose retelling of it in this chapter.

The third and most famous of Nizami's books, *Layla and Majnun,* is 4,500 lines long. This may rightly be called the Persian *Romeo and Juliet,* although actually it was written hundreds of years before Shakespeare's play. We present our retelling in this chapter.

Nizami's other three books of *mathnawi* are *Haft Paykar* (Seven Beauties), *Sharafnameh* (The Letter of Dignity), and *Eghbalnameh* (The Letter of Luck). The first is made up of seven fables about the life of Bahram, an Iranian king. The second and third describe the battles and conquests of Alexander the Great (Iskandar). Our last tale in this chapter is from this group of stories.

In addition to these six books, Nizami wrote a divan, or collection of poems (*ghazals* and *qasidas*). A large portion of this work seems to have been lost. As is true of so many of the early Sufi masters, what survives intact of Nizami is his teachings. This in itself serves as a reminder to the seeker to recognize the transitory nature of worldly life.

KHUSRAU AND SHIRIN

Shapur was tired from an all-night party with the young prince, Khusrau. Shapur had been trying to arrange a suitable match for Khusrau, and he felt satisfied with the night's efforts. "I used the oldest trick in the book," he thought, grinning to himself as he climbed into bed, "and Khusrau fell for it! So much the better for him." On a more serious note, Shapur reflected, "Well, it's about time he found someone and settled down. How long can he continue to lead an irresponsible life devoted to pleasure?"

What this loyal cousin and courtier of the prince had done was to vividly describe a young princess he had once seen while visiting Armenia. By the end of the party, Khusrau was so intrigued by the enchanting description of the princess that he had fallen in love with a mere image. Yet even Shapur was amazed by the description that had come from his own lips; it hardly seemed that he could have created so alluring a vision.

The object of Khusrau's fantasies, Shirin, had no idea of Shapur's plan. Neither would she have cared, had she known about it. This young lady was far too independent to let a matter such as marriage disturb her thoughts. Perhaps it was just this free spirit of hers that made her so attractive. She was brought up as the only heir to the throne of Armenia. Her aunt, Mahin, the Great Queen, had no children of her own, so Shirin was her successor. Perhaps that was why she devoted her energies to learning skills that women of her time usually took no interest in, such as riding, hunting, and martial arts.

It was not that Shirin had no feminine qualities. On the contrary, she was unusually lovely: shining, ocean-blue eyes; cheeks so red as to appear almost unnatural, given her fair skin; thick, dark curls that danced wildly about her face. So great was her beauty, in fact, that Shapur's superlatives had been no exaggeration. The prince had become so desirous of seeing Shirin that Shapur had agreed to set out at once for Armenia and bring the princess back with him.

Summer, with its glorious weather and blooming flowers, had brought a happy spirit to Armenia. A habit of Shirin's in this season was to spend all day long in the countryside. Her own special place was a spot under a small waterfall surrounded by thick foliage, safe from the view of others, where she and her handmaidens could swim privately. Usually a group of her friends would accompany her as well.

When Shapur arrived at the Armenian capital, he received the news that the princess was camping outdoors. Immediately, he rode out to the countryside. On the way, he concocted a plan to attract Shirin's attention to Khusrau.

It was afternoon when Shapur came upon the royal camp. He

dismounted and walked near the camp without being noticed. For a while he watched the happy group from behind the trees. Then he looked around and finally found a walnut tree that was perfect for what he had in mind.

Shapur fetched a carefully rolled picture from his saddle bag and brought it to the tree. A talented artist, he had sketched a lifelike portrait of the handsome prince in a satin robe of dark blue ornamented with diamonds and sapphires, his right hand resting on the sword tucked through the thick satin belt around his waist. Khusrau's expressive black eyes looked directly into the viewer's eyes. A few careless black curls on his forehead gave him a devil-may-care look. With his perfect straight nose and his lips slightly pressed in hauteur, his picture was incredibly attractive.

Shapur posted the portrait on the tree and sat further away, waiting. At last, Shirin separated from her friends for a walk. She took her steps slowly, inhaling the cool breeze and the fresh smell of grass. As she drew close to the walnut tree, she stopped and closed her eyes, trying to free her thoughts from the past or future. Her mind clear, she meditated for a few minutes. With a smile, she opened her eyes—and beheld the picture hanging on the walnut tree. Curious, she approached the picture and examined it.

It was a drawing of the most handsome man she had ever seen. "Who can this be?" she thought. Taking the picture off the tree, she stared at it in confusion for a couple of minutes, feeling a kind of churning in her stomach. What was happening to her? She returned to the camp, the mysterious portrait tucked into her clothing. The walk she was supposed to be taking was forgotten. All the rest of the day, Shirin sat by the river, staring at the water. She spoke to no one; neither did she reply to her friends, who were surprised at this sudden change in her mood. "Come on, Shirin, what's the matter with you?" they said. "You look like you've seen a ghost." Instead of answering, Shirin went to her tent, took the picture out, and looked at it.

Shirin's Abigail knew her lady's different moods, but this one was unusual. Becoming curious, she kept a watch on her mistress from afar. When Shirin retired to her tent, Abigail followed her. Carefully she peeped into the tent and saw Shirin gazing at a drawing. When after a time Shirin fell asleep, the maid tiptoed in and pulled the picture slowly from under her lady's mattress.

Driven by an extreme concern for her mistress, Abigail took the picture to Shirin's friends and told them what she had seen. Following a discussion over the strange turn of events, the friends concluded that Shirin must have somehow become lovesick over a picture she had found. That same afternoon, they confronted her and advised her to forget the entire matter. "What if your aunt finds out?" one asked. "What are you going to tell her? That you have fallen in love with a picture?" But there was no use trying to talk Shirin out of her feelings. The picture had captured her heart.

How ironic that Shirin and Khusrau each fell in love with an image of the other—without ever having met!

Shirin returned to the tree several times in the hope of finding some information about the person in the picture. She asked her maids to look around and see what they could find.

The maids found Shapur, relaxing under a tree, a short distance from the camp. He was brought before the princess. After dismissing the servants, Shirin demanded who he was and what he was doing so close to the royal camp. Shapur introduced himself, reassured the princess of his respectability, and claimed that he was only a traveler passing through.

Shirin looked at Shapur through narrow eyes in a speculative way. "Someone has posted a strange picture on a nearby tree," she said, and presented the picture to Shapur. "Have you seen anyone around the area?"

Shapur looked at the picture with apparent surprise. "Why, this is a picture of Prince Khusrau of Persia!" He looked at Shirin with an expression of great admiration. "His majesty is the bravest of all men." He then put the picture down and said, "I have the honor of having being in his majesty's court and company for years. I am also a relation of his."

Forgetting her original purpose of finding out where the picture had come from, Shirin urged Shapur to tell her more about the prince. In much the same glowing way that he had described the young princess to Khusrau, Shapur spoke of his cousin to Shirin. He encouraged her to travel to Persia immediately to meet him. "I am confident that the prince would be honored to meet you, my lady."

Shirin thought quickly. Travel to Persia? But how could she explain to her aunt the reason for such a trip? What if she were to go by herself? She would think of some excuse and write her aunt once she was in Persia and had met her prince. Maybe by then she would have good news for her aunt as well! "I cannot let anyone know that I am going," she told Shapur, "for if I do, my aunt may send for me."

Shapur reassured her that he would distract the maids so that she could escape unnoticed. He would join her later and make sure no one was following them. He advised her to dress as a man for her safety. He would give her a set of his own clothing from his saddle pack.

And so Shirin rode away on her horse, Shabdiz, the best and fastest in all the land. No one could ever hope to catch up with her when she was riding Shabdiz! Even Shapur, who departed only a couple of hours after Shirin, was left miles behind. By the time Aunt Mahin discovered her absence, the young woman was already days away. And not a soul knew in which direction she had headed.

Back in Persia, King Hurmuz had gone on a short trip. Taking advantage of his father's absence, Khusrau decided to have new coins minted carrying his own image instead of the king's. When Hurmuz returned to Mada'in, the capital city, he became enraged at his son's brash action. "What did he think—'Now that Father's gone, I am the king of Persia'?" he said angrily to his advisor. "I want him out of the capital. He is never to come back here again!"

But even before the king's decree could be delivered, Khusrau had left for Armenia. His friends in court had warned him of the king's anger. Besides, he had run out of patience in waiting for news from Shapur. He decided to go after Shirin himself.

On the way, Khusrau stopped at a river to rest. Presently he sensed that he was not alone. Cautiously, he led his horse behind a bush, hiding himself too. A girl was swimming in the river. Her marble-carved body moved swiftly like a fish in the water, and her tousled hair clung wildly to her face and shoulders, giving her an unsophisticated kind of beauty. He caught his breath at the sight of this overwhelming creature. Somehow it seemed he had seen her before, but he could not remember where or when. As she emerged from the water and began to dress—surprisingly, in men's clothing—Khusrau turned his head, embarrassed to look at her naked body.

At the sound of a horse whinnying, the prince turned back— only to find that the girl had vanished as quickly as a breeze. He rode all around the area but could find no sign of her. "What kind of horse could run that fast?" he wondered.

The prince still had quite a few miles to go before arriving at Armenia's capital when he noticed a rider in the distance. It was Shapur. Khusrau greeted him with pleasure and recounted to him the events that had taken place in his absence, and added that he was on his way to ask Mahin for asylum. Shapur, in turn, told him the news of Shirin's escape to Persia. Khusrau realized then that it must have been Shirin he had glimpsed swimming in the river.

But alas, there was no going back there now that Khusrau had enraged his father. Without his father's support and protection, his life would be threatened by opportunist courtiers. For some time now he had suspected a few of the court officers of plotting against the throne, but he had been unable to present proof to his father. To make matters worse, Khusrau's own absence from the court would make it easy for the plotters to attack the king. Khusrau feared the worst, but he would have to stay away for a while. Once his father's anger had dissipated, he would return and apologize to him. Khusrau rode on toward Armenia.

When Shirin arrived at Mada'in, she learned that the prince had fled. What would she do now? On the one hand, she regretted having come, but on the other, she did not have the temerity to go back and face her aunt. When King Hurmuz was informed of the Armenian princess's identity and reason for coming to Persia, he treated her with the utmost kindness—even ordering a mansion to be built for her on Khusrau's estate near Mada'in. A large number of maids were appointed to serve her. And so Shirin settled into her big new house with hundreds of maids, but with a lonely heart.

In Armenia, Mahin received Khusrau and Shapur warmly. The prince resided in a royal villa. When he felt certain that Shirin would not return on her own, he sent Shapur to Iran to bring her back to Armenia. But fate had another game in store for the hapless lovers. Not more than a day after Shapur had left, a messenger arrived from Persia with the news that King Hurmuz had died. Khusrau was awaited back in Mada'in to claim the throne. He thus prepared to leave.

In the short time that he had known Shirin before his death, King Hurmuz had developed a fondness for her lively wit and humor, and she in turn had enjoyed his company and fatherly support. Upon his death, Shirin felt lonelier than ever.

Some of Khusrau's servants were sent to Shirin's mansion, but the maids provided little companionship. These women, who had been the objects of the prince's flirtations in the past, despised Shirin, thinking that Khusrau might fall in love with her when the two met. Driven by jealousy, they made it a point to create small inconveniences for Shirin. Their malicious jokes ranged from making her bathwater too hot or too cold to "accidentally" tearing the hem of her dress, to concealing a dead mouse in her food. Although the unsuspecting Shirin tried to take control of such situations, by the time everything fell into place, her day had already been ruined, and she would feel sad and homesick.

At times like this, Shirin regretted her decision not to inform her aunt of her whereabouts or to explain her impulsive departure from Armenia. What excuse could she give for staying here, especially now that the prince was not in Persia? In time, she wished she had never left home. And so, by the time Shapur arrived at her mansion to take her back to Armenia, Shirin was more than ready to return.

Alas, neither of them realized that Khusrau was on his way to Persia. They rode to Armenia, missing Khusrau because he had taken a shortcut and not the main road.

Mahin, who was relieved to see her niece safe and sound, welcomed her back with open arms. Shirin then explained to her aunt the reason for her flight. "Fate plays funny games," Mahin responded. "All the time that you were looking for your prince, he was here. And now that you are here, he is in Persia." She reflected for a moment. "Whatever may happen, I want you to promise me one thing." Shirin nodded her assent. "Promise me that when the day finally comes that you meet this prince, you will be very cautious about becoming involved with him. I am afraid that he is after the pleasures of life. This worries me." With a wave of her hand she stopped Shirin from interrupting. "Yes, I know he is a capable, impressive, and handsome young man, but if you ever do meet him, you must never agree to anything less than marriage with him." It was clear that Mahin would not tolerate any objection to what she had just said, so Shirin obediently promised her aunt.

A few days after Khusrau's arrival in Mada'in, he was crowned. Although he had attained the heights of worldly power, he could hardly concentrate on his moment of glory, so restless was he with thoughts of Shirin. When would he see her?

Among the officers of the royal court, there was one Bahram, a general who did not want Khusrau in power and did not approve of his ways of governing. Bahram wrote letters to the top-ranking officers of the army, accusing Khusrau of having had his own father murdered in cold blood in order to seize the throne, and asserting that he did not know how to take care of the country and its affairs. He added that, according to rumors, Khusrau was in love with some foreign girl—clearly, he implied, romantic dalliance was all the young king was capable of. Bahram then suggested a military coup to rid the country of this ineffectual and dangerous youth. The officers agreed, and soon the army, under the leadership of Bahram, took over the capital city. Khusrau, who found himself without support from his father's friends, fled to Armenia, where he knew he would find welcome. In his place, Bahram sat on the throne.

The news of the Persian upheaval had reached Armenia. Shirin had been worried about Khusrau, but Shapur was able to reassure her, for he had become a dear friend and confidant to the princess. "Do not fear for his majesty's safety," Shapur had said; "he is too smart to let any harm come to himself."

To occupy his friend with more happy thoughts, Shapur had suggested a deer-hunting trip, knowing it was a favorite pastime for the princess. Thus, Shirin, accompanied by Shapur and a few servants, camped some fifteen miles outside the Armenian capital. On the second day Shirin pointed out a rider approaching in the distance. Only when he drew near did Shapur recognize Khusrau, dressed in a white peasant outfit. After so much longing and waiting, Khusrau and Shirin at last stood before each other. But the meeting was so sudden and unexpected that they could only mumble shy greetings upon being introduced.

Khusrau rode with the group out into the countryside to camp at Shirin's favorite spot. Attended by the musicians and servants in Shirin's entourage, they spent days singing and dancing, drinking, and playing polo. Of course, the rapt young lovers had no notion of how much time had passed.

After some days, Khusrau and Shirin were finally able to be alone, far from the sight of the others. Under the same walnut tree that once displayed Khusrau's mysterious portrait, they kissed and declared their love for each other. But when Khusrau asked Shirin to spend the night with him, she took a step backward. "I thought you loved me," she said reproachfully.

"But I do," Khusrau answered. "That is why I want to be with you."

Biting her lip, Shirin tried to conceal her anger, but her voice shook. "This is not love, it is lust! If you really loved me, you would first oust that intruder, Bahram, and take back the country that is rightly yours—and then ask for my hand."

Khusrau was so stung by her cutting words that he could only reply, "Don't you know that it was my love for you that made me abandon my country and come here?" Then, with a sigh, he returned to camp, mounted his horse, and rode away.

Khusrau did not stop riding until he reached Rome. There he sought the help of the Roman emperor to get his country back from Bahram. The emperor, impressed with Khusrau's youth and abilities, gave him his daughter, Maryam, in marriage, and sent the royal troops with him to Persia. In a matter of days, Khusrau's army recaptured Persia, killed the treacherous Bahram, and regained the throne.

After Khusrau's brusque departure, Shirin was filled with regret, wishing a thousand times that she had been kinder to her beloved. But it was too late; now she was alone again, with only Shapur to comfort her. He listened patiently to her endless laments and became the companion of her sorrow—a sorrow that was com-

pounded when Mahin, who had been like a mother to Shirin, died
of pneumonia.

Now Shirin was crowned queen. This responsibility was the last
thing she wanted, but what choice did she have? She had just begun
to immerse herself in the affairs of her country when she received
the final blow: the news came that Khusrau had taken his throne
back, but at his side was another woman. Maryam, the Roman
princess, was now his wife. Shirin was devastated. Yet, in the midst
of her tears, her heart rejoiced that Khusrau had reclaimed his
rightful place as the king of Persia.

Eventually Shirin found her separation from Khusrau unbearable. Not even her royal duties could distract her from her misery.
She felt like a stranger in her own land and unable to perform her
obligation to her people. Thus, after consulting with Shapur, she
decided to leave the country, abandoning the affairs of state to her
only cousin. And so she moved to Persia.

Shirin had a mansion built for herself near Mada'in, where she
could hear news of Khusrau every day. She also had independent
quarters built for Shapur, who had accompanied her to Persia.

As soon as Khusrau heard that Shirin was living nearby, the
sleeping flame of his love for her sprang to life once again. His
informers brought him the details of Shirin's life in response to his
inquiry. Having made a decision, he informed his wife: "My dear,
I would like to have Queen Shirin moved to a palace." Assuming a
serious expression, Khusrau tried his best not to betray his deep
feelings. "I am told she has but a handful of servants, and that her
home is not suitable for one of her rank." Khusrau looked into
Maryam's searching eyes with a softness she rarely observed in
him. "It would be considered inhospitable of me to let a queen live
in so humble a condition. She is royalty, and the thought of allowing my guest to be treated any less than she deserves disturbs me."
He smiled with this last remark, hoping to convince his wife that
he cared only about preserving his own honor.

Maryam had heard the rumors concerning her husband's love for Shirin and was not fooled by Khusrau's poor acting ability. She began to cry violently, accusing Khusrau of not loving her and of scheming to have a secret romance with the Armenian queen. "There is nothing improper and dishonorable about allowing her to live the way she has chosen to. If she wanted to live like royalty, she would have remained in her own country, would she not?" she challenged. "Besides," Maryam added, "she has not taken any steps to pay her respects to the king and queen, so she must wish to be left alone." When Khusrau did not respond to her tears or her arguments, she angrily advanced toward him, her finger raised in a forbidding manner, and threatened, "If I ever find out that you have taken so much as a single step to see Shirin, I will kill myself. I swear it!"

Never again did Khusrau mention Shirin's name in the presence of his wife, yet he secretly sent word to his beloved, pleading for a meeting. But Shirin refused to meet him and sent back a terse message: "You had better remain faithful to your wife."

The long days and nights that she spent thinking and worrying about the king finally took their toll on Shirin, who became ill and weak. The royal physicians prescribed goat's milk, but the only available herds were in the mountains. Who would bring her the milk from such a distance? Shapur had an idea: there was an architect and artist named Farhad who lived nearby. Surely this clever person would have the answer. Shapur invited him to Shirin's villa and explained Shirin's plight. Could Farhad think of a way to get the goat's milk quickly to Shirin? When the young architect beheld Shirin, he fell in love with her at first sight. Inflamed with a new enthusiasm for the task entrusted to him, he vowed to bring the milk to Shirin, no matter what it would take.

The tall, handsome Farhad was one of the strongest men in the land. He lived honestly and cared nothing for wealth or material things. If he designed a building or other structure, he was motivated solely by his interest in that particular job or a desire to help people who needed his work and talent. Now that he had found a new passion, he took his tools and went to the mountains with no delay. In a matter of weeks, the great architect had designed and built a channel that ran from the mountains directly to Shirin's villa. The shepherds milked their many goats, and a stream of milk flowed down virtually to Shirin's door!

To show her appreciation for Farhad's labor of love, Shirin invited him to her mansion and thanked him in person. After praising his work, she took off her earrings and handed them to Farhad, saying, "You will always be dear to me. I shall never forget you. Please accept as a token of my friendship these earrings, which are all that I have left of the wealth I abandoned when I left Armenia."

To Farhad, this precious gift was more than he could ever wish for. He carried the earrings with him wherever he went, and became so drunk with love for Shirin that he spent days at a time alone in the mountains, imbibing nourishment from the milk stream. Sometimes he would walk near Shirin's house, hoping to glimpse her. He spoke openly to people of his feelings, and soon everyone in Mada'in knew of Farhad's devotion to Shirin.

Khusrau was no exception. He had commanded that Farhad be brought before him, and now he was impatiently pacing the great hall in which he was to receive the architect. Hard as he tried, he could not control an apprehension about losing Shirin to the man he was about to meet. When his counselor announced Farhad, he turned on his heel to face the visitor.

Farhad executed a graceful bow and, slowly straightening up, looked at the king, waiting to be addressed.

"You are Farhad, the architect?" At the nod of confirmation, Khusrau motioned for Farhad to sit down. "I have heard about you," he said, continuing to walk past the young man now seated on the floor cushions, his eyes downcast. "Where are you from?"

Much to the king's dismay, Farhad showed no sign of discomfort. The fact that he was in the presence of His Majesty the King of Persia did not impress him. Calmly, he lifted his head and looked at Khusrau. "If Your Majesty means where was I born, I must say that I was born in Mada'in. But ever since I have fallen in love, my home is wherever my beloved lives."

A grim look passed over the king's face like a shadow. No one had been bold enough to talk to the king in such a manner. Yet the young man had an honest quality about him. "I have been informed of your services for Her Highness the Queen of Armenia. Is it true that you have taken a fancy to Her Highness?"

Farhad nodded. "It is true that I love Her Highness enough to dedicate my life to her."

"That is absurd." Khusrau clenched his teeth and looked directly into Farhad's eyes. "You cannot expect this infatuation to last."

"To Your Majesty it may look like a mere infatuation, but for me it is true love," Farhad replied. "And true love has no end. Although it may seem to end with the lover's physical death, in reality it will last into eternity."

For the first time in his life Khusrau had met his match. To compete with this fellow would be a challenge indeed. Taking a deep breath, he turned his back to Farhad, trying to gain control over his anger. "What about *her* feelings? Have you considered what Her Highness's wishes may be? And what if she asks you for something you do not possess, or demands a feat that is not in your power to perform?"

"I do not expect her to return my love; I ask only to be allowed to love her." Farhad moved in his seat and began to rise with Khusrau's nod. "My heart, my only possession, already belongs to her," he said, now face to face with the king, "and if she desires more of me, I beg God to grant me the power to fulfill her wishes."

Khusrau motioned to the servants to pour two cups of wine, and he handed one to Farhad. "My friend," he said, smiling for the first time, "it seems to me that your life is one of pain and trouble." He sipped at his wine and put a hand on Farhad's shoulder, directing him toward the great window that overlooked the garden. "Why should you want to live a life where your beloved does not so much as acknowledge your existence, when you can have all the love you desire from other beautiful women? Why should you live in poverty and misery, when you can have all the money and wealth you desire?"

Farhad understood what Khusrau was suggesting, but if he was angry, he showed no sign of it. Calmly he turned to the king. "I do not consider my life one of pain, because for a man who truly loves, pain and its remedy are one and the same. And the fact that my beloved does or does not acknowledge me is of no consequence. I love her for her own sake and not for my own. It is enough for me to love her. And as far as my desires are concerned, how can I have any desires, when I am hardly aware of myself anymore?"

"What if your king commands you to leave Her Highness and abandon this foolish love?"

Farhad knew that Khusrau had once loved Shirin, but had not realized until now that he was still very much in love with her. He suddenly felt a sympathy for the king. "That I cannot obey, sire," he said, with a glint of sadness in his eyes.

The longer the conversation went on, the more defeated Khusrau felt. He therefore dismissed Farhad and summoned his advisors. "He is a dangerous man," Khusrau said. "We could not bribe him with anything." Khusrau's brow furrowed. "We should think of a way to get him out of the way."

The sages conferred briefly and announced their solution, and Khusrau called once again for Farhad. "We will promise not to come between you and Shirin on one condition," pronounced the king.

The young architect jumped to his feet, tears of happiness rolling down his face. "Whatever the great king desires!"

"We need a passage carved through the Mountain of Bistun, so that we can travel to the other side more quickly and efficiently."

For years, Bistun Mountain had been a formidable obstacle. All efforts to construct a tunnel had failed, for the solid granite of the hill would not allow workers to make any headway. No one had yet been able to surmount the hardships of such a project. Khusrau smiled to himself. Once Farhad was embarked on this impossible task, there would be no chance of his return.

"Once you finish the job to our satisfaction, we will give you Shirin's hand in marriage," Khusrau said.

"I will start tomorrow. And I will do the job to the best of my ability," Farhad replied, happy in the thought that Shirin would soon be his.

For Farhad, that Bistun project was no hardship. Dreaming of his beloved as he toiled made the work go easily for him. He did not notice the hot sun, his aching muscles, or his sore back. Every stroke of the hammer sounded to him like a sweet word from Shirin. At the end of the day, when he quit work, he carved images of Shirin, Khusrau, and himself in the stone. The progress of his work on the carvings mirrored the progress of his labor on the mountain.

Shirin, upon hearing of Farhad's undertaking, knew instantly that it was a plan intended for his demise. She realized that she must ride out to Bistun and warn her friend.

They talked for a while. Farhad showed her his work. The job was more than half done, and she decided not to tell him of Khusrau's plan after all. "Khusrau will be defeated by his own plot," she thought.

The same day, Shirin returned home with a conviction of certain victory. But her visit with Farhad had not gone unnoticed. The king's spies took the news to him. Panic-stricken, the king gathered his advisors. On the one hand, he was afraid that Shirin might be falling in love with Farhad—why else would she take the trouble to visit him? On the other hand, now that the construction of the Bistun tunnel was nearly finished, what was he to do about his promise to Farhad? He had sorely underestimated the determined lover.

Khusrau liked the new idea his advisors presented to him. Accordingly, he sent an old man to Bistun Mountain. The man greeted Farhad with a long face. "What are you doing to this mountain?" he asked.

Farhad explained his task, adding, "For my love, no effort is too difficult." He struck the ground with his hammer. "I would move the mountain itself if I had to!"

The old man shook his head sadly. "What a pity . . . ," he said, turning his face as if to hide a tear. The gesture did not go unnoticed by Farhad.

"What do you mean?" Farhad asked, putting the hammer aside.

"Nothing." The old man seemed reluctant to talk.

"You must tell me."

"I cannot help thinking that you are working so hard . . . and for what?"

Farhad took the old man by the shoulders. "Please, tell me what you know!"

"Your beloved is dead," the old man blurted out with anger and grief. "Shirin passed away a couple of days ago."

Farhad released the old man's shoulders and sank to the ground, stunned.

Night fell. The old man was long gone. Farhad had not budged from his position.

Little by little, he was dying inside. He had no energy left to stand up. It was as if all the physical labor of the past months had suddenly taken its toll on his body. He dragged himself through the dirt until he reached the portrait of Shirin that he had carved.

His hands, full of blisters and bruises, started to bleed as he caressed her image, leaving his blood on her face. Then he pressed his face in misery against the stony face of Shirin.

The next day, Khusrau had Farhad's lifeless body removed from Bistun and buried in a simple grave nearby.

Shirin mourned Farhad's death for several days. Khusrau wrote her a letter of sympathy, which she answered with these words: "You deprived us of a dear friend. I pray that God will forgive your soul."

Soon the memory of Farhad faded from people's minds. Life continued as usual. Shirin's love for Khusrau was stronger than ever—so strong, in fact, that she forgave him for what he had done to Farhad. Shirin was still in love with Khusrau, and Khusrau was still in love with her. Neither saw the other, but each always asked for news of the other from friends.

Once again tragedy struck when Maryam, the queen, became moribund with a sudden illness and, soon after, passed away. After the period of mourning was over, Shirin sent her condolences to Khusrau, adding, "Even though the queen is gone now, there is no need for the king to worry. I am sure His Majesty can find comfort in the arms of many available young ladies." Furious at this taunt, Khusrau made no reply. Instead, he took up her suggestion and did just that.

For a couple of years Khusrau amused himself with a variety of pretty girls. But eventually his anger cooled, and he regretted his rash actions. He remembered his old friend and relative Shapur, who had been Shirin's companion for years, and let him know that he wished to see him.

Shapur arranged a private meeting with the king in his quarters. He had Shirin wait in an adjoining room. In reply to the king's urgent questions about Shirin, Shapur assured him that she had not stopped loving him and had not let any other man into her heart. Shirin followed the news of the king every day, Shapur declared, just waiting for the moment when she could see him again. "I know you better than you do yourself," Shapur told Khusrau. "I know you love her, too. But, like her, you are too proud and too stubborn to admit to it." He walked toward the king. "Come, now, it is time you saw Shirin. You owe her an apology." Before the king could utter a reply, Shirin stepped into the room. Shapur quietly took his leave, closing the door behind him.

The anger and despair of many years seemed to vanish as the two lovers fell into each other's arms. Khusrau and Shirin talked of all they had been through during their time of separation. And then Khusrau knelt before Shirin and humbly asked her to be his queen.

The next day, Shirin was escorted to the capital. Six maids helped her dress for the sumptuous wedding. The entire city was invited to witness the magical moment of union as Shirin and Khusrau knelt before the high priest. At last, they were joined in marriage. The wedding celebration went on joyously for days.

Shirin gave the throne of Armenia to Shapur and became King Khusrau's wisest advisor. The people loved her and freely came to her with their troubles. She listened to them and made recommendations to Khusrau. Never before had Persia witnessed such a period of prosperity.

But there was one dark spot in this bright picture. It was Shirvieh, Khusrau's son from his marriage with Maryam. This boy had been devious from childhood, and Khusrau feared him. Therefore, acting on the counsel of his advisors, the king had not declared Shirvieh his heir to the throne. Shirvieh could not stand seeing his father happy in marriage and popular among the people. For a long time, he had nourished a grudge, blaming his mother's death on Khusrau's negligence. To make matters worse, as a passionate young man himself, Shirvieh could not resist Shirin's beauty and had fallen in love with her. All these grievances led the spiteful young man to secretly plot against his father.

To develop a foundation in the king's court, he paid off a few men there and promised them wealth and position should he ever come to power. He carefully gathered people around him by going to public places in the guise of an ordinary man, posing as a friend of the common folk. Even though the king never gave his comments and suggestions serious consideration in the court, Shirvieh managed to give the public the impression that it was *he* who had defended the rights of the poor in court, that it was *his* efforts that had improved the lot of the common people.

Having thus ingratiated himself to both the people and the courtiers, Shirvieh put the crowning touch on his scheme: he and his followers took Khusrau and Shirin prisoner in their own palace. The evil son then sat on the throne and declared himself king.

Oddly enough, the king made no effort to take back his throne. Together with his queen, he lived in contentment in the simple room in which they had been confined.

Seeing such happpiness was a crushing defeat for Shirvieh. In his desire for Shirin, he had imagined that she, wanting to remain queen, would come to the new king willingly. To his dismay, Shirin stayed faithful to her love. It was unbearable for him to see her always in his father's arms. And so he busied himself with a new scheme.

It was past midnight. The full moon was out, no sound could be heard, and peace pervaded the palace. Shirvieh quietly opened the door to the room where the captives were held. Shirin and Khusrau were sleeping peacefully next to each other. He looked at his father's face for a few minutes. He could feel the anger rising in him. Shivering, he clenched his teeth and pulled his dagger out of its sheath. He held it above Khusrau's body for a moment and then plunged the knife into his father's heart. Immediately, he ran toward the door and left the room.

Khusrau awakened in horror with a searing pain in his chest. He knew he was dying, but he did not want to frighten Shirin, so he bit his lip, enduring the agony until he could no longer keep his eyes open. Moments later, the wetness of Khusrau's blood caused Shirin to awaken. But it was too late, for her beloved husband was already dead—murdered in cold blood.

It was not hard for Shirin to guess who the murderer was, but she said nothing. To all appearances, it was a calm and resigned Shirin who graciously accepted Shirvieh's proposal of marriage. She asked only that she be given time to hold a respectable funeral for Khusrau.

Shirin secretly gave all her belongings to the poor, keeping only her best dress and jewelry, which she wore on the day of the funeral. When she joined the crowd of ladies in the procession, people were startled to see her beautifully made up and attractively attired. Was this the proper behavior of a grieving widow? To make matters worse, the queen danced all the way to the graveyard! Evidently she was happy about her husband's death—either that, or she had lost her mind altogether!

In Khusrau's burial chamber, Shirin asked their friends to give her a moment alone so that she could bid farewell to her husband. When everyone had left the chamber, Shirin stood quietly and respectfully at Khusrau's side, staring at her husband's closed eyes. Then, calmly, she reached under her dress and pulled out something she had hidden there. With closed eyes, Shirin thrust the knife into her own heart without hesitation. She then stumbled to her husband's body and, laying her head on her beloved's chest, died with a smile on her lips.

AFTERWORD

It is not clear whether the events recounted in *Khusrau and Shirin* actually took place at some point in history, or whether they were a product of Nizami's imagination. However, there was a Persian king named Khusrau who ruled during the Sassanid dynasty, contemporary with the Prophet Muhammad. There is also a historical monument, a carving of two men and a woman, at the Mountain of Bistun near the city of Kirmanshah in western Iran. The carving has been restored, and today the Bistun attracts many Middle Eastern tourists. The artwork has become famous, winning the admiration of artists, lovers of beauty, and all who are inspired by the mysterious romantic theme it suggests.

LAYLA AND MAJNUN

The chief of the Bani 'Umar tribe of Arabia had everything a man could want, except for one thing—if only he had a child. The medicine men of the village suggested many potions and medicines, but to no avail. When nothing seemed to work, his wife suggested that the couple kneel before God's altar and, in sincerity, ask the dear Lord to grant them this boon. "Why not?" replied the chief. "We have tried almost all other ways. One more will not hurt."

So the man and wife knelt in front of the Almighty, shedding tears from the depth of their wounded hearts. "O Dearest of All, let not our tree be fruitless. Let us taste the sweetness of carrying a baby in our arms. Grant us the responsibility of raising a good human being. Give us the chance to make You proud of our child."

Before too long, their prayer was heard, and the Lord granted them a baby boy, whom they named Qays. The father's happiness was boundless, for Qays was a boy loved by all, a beautiful child, with big brown eyes and black hair, who was constantly the center of attention and admiration. From the beginning, Qays showed exceptional intelligence and physical ability. He had an unusual talent for learning the warrior's arts as well as a gift for music, poetry, and painting.

When it was time for the lad to go to school, his father decided to build a school where only the best teachers of Arabia would teach, and only the cream of the crop would study. The sons and daughters of noble families came from all over Arabia to attend the new school.

Among them was the daughter of the chief of a neighboring tribe—a jewel of a girl, possessed of remarkable feminine beauty. Her hair and eyes were black as night; for this reason they had named her Layla—"the Night." Although she was only twelve, many men had already pleaded for her hand in marriage, for, as was the custom in those times, girls were often betrothed at as young as the age of nine.

Layla and Qays were classmates, and from their first day at school they were drawn to each other. As time passed, this spark of attraction grew into a burning flame of love. For them, school was no longer a place to learn—now it was simply a place to meet each other. While the teacher discoursed, they stared at each other, and when it was time to write their lessons, they wrote instead each other's names on the paper. No other friend, no other pleasure existed for them. The world had become only Qays and Layla; they were deaf and blind to all else.

Little by little, everybody came to know of their love, and tongues began to wag. Now, in those days, it was not proper for a girl to be known as the object of someone's love—and certainly not to respond to it. When Layla's parents heard the whisperings about their daughter, they forbade her to go to school. The burden of shame for the family of a chief of the tribe was more than they could bear.

When Layla failed to appear in the classroom, Qays became so distressed that he left school and began to wander the streets in search of his beloved, calling out her name. He composed poetry for her and recited it as he walked the streets. He spoke of nothing but Layla, nor did he respond to others unless they asked a question about her. People laughed and pointed, saying, "Look at him—he's a *majnun*, a madman!," and the name stuck.

Seeing people, listening to them, or speaking with them had

become unbearable to Majnun. He wished to see no one but Layla. And so he abandoned his own village for hers. He knew that she had been imprisoned in her house by her parents, who wisely recognized that if Layla were left free to go where she wished, she would certainly go to Majnun. Majnun found a place on the mountaintop near Layla's village and built a cottage for himself with a view of her house.

All day long Majnun would sit in front of his cottage, beside a small stream winding its way down toward the village. He spoke to the water, sending wildflower petals with its flow, believing that it would carry his message of love to Layla. He addressed the birds, asking them to fly to Layla and let her know he was near. He inhaled the wind that blew from the west, for it had passed through Layla's town. If a stray dog happened to come by from her village, he would feed it and take care of it, loving the animal as if it were sacred, respecting it and keeping it until the time the dog chose to leave, if indeed it did so. Anything that came from the place of his beloved was as cherished and dear to him as the beloved herself.

Months passed, and Majnun had seen not a trace of Layla. His longing for her was so great that he felt he could not survive another day without seeing her again. Sometimes his former companions from school came to visit, but he talked to them only of Layla, of how much he missed her. One day, three boys who came by were so touched by Majnun's agony that they determined to help him see Layla again.

Their plan was a clever one. The next day, they and Majnun approached Layla's house, disguised as women. They easily passed as her maids and managed to reach the door to her room. Majnun entered the room while the others stayed outside, standing guard.

From the day she stopped going to school, Layla had done nothing but think of Qays. Strangely enough, anytime she heard birds singing through the window or the wind blowing gently, she closed her eyes, thinking she could hear Qays's voice in them. She would catch the flower petals brought by the wind or the stream and know that they had come from Qays. But never did she speak to anyone, not even her best friends, about her love.

The day that Majnun entered Layla's room, she had sensed his coming. She was dressed in her loveliest garment, a long turquoise silk dress. Her hair was unbraided and carefully combed around her shoulders. Her eyes were penciled, in the custom of Arab women, with a black powder called *surmeh*. Her lips were reddened, and her naturally rosy cheeks were glowing, betraying her excitement. She sat in front of the door, waiting. When Majnun entered, Layla remained seated, for even though she had been told he would come, she could not believe it had really happened.

Majnun stood by the door for several minutes, drinking in the sight of Layla. At last they were together again! Nothing could be heard but the sound of the two lovers' hearts beating. They stared and stared at each other, unaware of the passage of time.

One of the household maids noticed the unknown women outside her mistress's room. Her suspicion aroused, she alerted one of the guards. But by the time Layla's mother came to investigate, Majnun and his friends were long gone. However, once her parents had questioned Layla, it was not difficult for them to figure out what had happened. Her silence and the happiness in her eyes told all.

After that, Layla's father had guards stationed at every door in the house. There was no way Majnun could find access to even the most remote part of the house. But if her father thought that by taking this precaution he could change the way they felt about each other, he was sadly in error.

When Majnun's father learned of the incident in Layla's house, he decided to put an end to the drama by asking her father for Layla's hand for his son. He prepared a caravan of gifts and set out for Layla's village.

The guest was well received, and the two chiefs talked of the happiness of their children. Majnun's father spoke first: "You know well, my friend, that there are two things essential to happiness—love and wealth. My son loves your daughter, and I can assure you that I would give them enough money to provide them with a comfortable life."

"I have nothing against Qays, and I believe you, for you are without doubt an honorable man," Layla's father replied. 'However, you cannot blame me for being cautious about your son. Everyone knows of his abnormal behavior. He dresses like a beggar. He must not have taken a bath in ages. He lives with animals and shuns people. Tell me, my friend, if you had a daughter and I were in your place, would you give your daughter to my son?"

No argument came from Qays's father. What could he say? That at one time his son had been a model of excellence for his peers? That he was the smartest and most talented young man in the entire land of Arabia? Of course not. Even the father himself had a hard time believing any of that anymore. It had been a long time since anyone had heard a sentence that made any sense from Majnun. "I am not going to stand by and watch my son destroy himself," he thought. "I must do something."

When the chief returned home, he sent for his son. He arranged a dinner in his honor to which the most beautiful girls of the land were invited. Surely they would divert Majnun's attention from Layla, he thought.

At the party, Majnun was quiet, ignoring the other guests. He sat in a corner, looking at the girls only to search each one's features for similarities to his Layla's. One girl was wearing a dress similar to one of Layla's; another had hair as long as hers, and another a similar smile. But none was quite like her; none was even half as beautiful. The party only deepened Majnun's feelings for his beloved, and he grew distraught, blaming everyone at the party for trying to trick him. In tears, Majnun accused his parents and friends of being cruel and ruthless. So violent did his crying become that he finally dropped to the floor unconscious.

After this disaster, Qays's father decided to try taking the youth on a pilgrimage to Mecca in the hope that God might have mercy on him and free him from this devastating love. There, to please his father, Majnun knelt in front of the altar—but what did he pray? "O Dearest of All, King of Kings, You Who bestow love, I beg of You only one thing: to elevate me in love to such a degree that even though I may perish, my love and my beloved will thrive." The chief knew then that there was nothing he could do for his son.

After the pilgrimage, Majnun, who was unwilling to face the villagers, went to the mountains without telling anyone of his whereabouts. He did not return to his cottage, but instead chose a ruined building isolated from society, and resided there.

After that, no one heard from Majnun. His parents sent friends and relatives in search of him, but no one could find him. Many concluded that he had been killed by desert animals.

One day, a man who was passing by the ruined building noticed a strange figure sitting by one of the crumbling walls—a wild man with hair down to his shoulders, his beard long and untidy, his clothes torn and faded. When the passerby received no reply to his greeting, he approached the man. It was then that he noticed a wolf sleeping at the man's feet. "Hush," said the wild man, "lest you awaken my friend." Then he turned his gaze toward some distant point.

The curious traveler sat there quietly, waiting to see what would happen. Finally the wild man began to talk. Quickly the traveler learned that this was the famous Majnun, whose strange exploits were gossiped about all over Arabia. Apparently, Majnun had had no difficulty adapting to life in the wild. In fact, he had adjusted so well that it was hard not to see him as a natural part of the landscape. Animals were drawn to him, instinctively knowing that he was no harm to them. His kindness had earned their trust, even from the most notorious beast, such as the wolf. The traveler listened as Majnun sang his praises of Layla. They shared a piece of bread that the traveler had with him, and afterward the traveler took his leave and continued on his way.

When the traveler arrived at Majnun's village, he told people the story. Ultimately, word reached the chief, who invited the traveler to his house and asked for details. Overjoyed that Majnun was alive, the chief set out for the desert to find him.

At the sight of the ruins that the traveler had described, the chief was overcome with emotion. So this was the pathetic state to which his son had fallen. "O God, I beg of You to save my son and return him to his family," the chief cried out. Majnun heard his father's prayer and came rushing out of his hiding place. Dropping at his feet, he cried, "Dear Father, forgive me for all the pain I have caused you. Please forget that you ever had a son, for this may make it easier for you to overcome your grief. This is my fate—to love, and to live for love."

Father and son held each other and cried. It was to be their last meeting.

Layla's relatives blamed her father for mishandling the situation. They believed that the scandal had shamed the entire family. For this reason, Layla's parents confined her to her room. Some of her friends were allowed to visit, but she did not want any company. She turned inward, nourishing the flame of love that burned within.

To express her deepest feelings, she wrote poems to her beloved on small scraps of paper. Then, when she was permitted to spend some time alone in the garden, she would release these scraps to the wind. Villagers who found the air-borne poems took them to Majnun, and in this way, the two lovers were able to have some contact.

Since Majnun was known throughout the land, many people

went to visit him, but they stayed only a short while, for they knew he could not bear the company of people for very long. They listened to him sing beautiful verses and play enchantingly on his reed pipe. Some felt sorry for him; others were simply curious about his story. Yet everyone was able to sense his profound loving-kindness toward all creation.

One of these visitors was a brave knight called 'Amr, who had come upon Majnun in the course of his journey to Mecca. Although he had heard the famous love story in his town, he was eager to hear it from the lips of Majnun himself. The tragic drama of the tale so overwhelmed him with sorrow and sadness that he vowed to do whatever possible to help unite the two lovers—even if it meant destroying those who stood in their way!

Back at his hometown, 'Amr grimly gathered his troops. The army galloped into Layla's village and attacked the tribe without mercy. Defenders quickly arose, and many men were killed or injured. As 'Amr's troops were close to winning the battle, Layla's father sent a message to 'Amr: "If you or any of your soldiers want my daughter, I will give her up without a fight. Even if you want to kill her, I won't protest. But one thing I will never accept: do not ask me to give her to that madman!"

On the battlefield, Majnun wandered freely among the warriors and attended to Layla's injured kinsmen. He tended them with utmost care and did whatever he could to ease their wounds. When 'Amr demanded an explanation for his aiding and abetting of the enemy, Majnun replied, "These people come from the land of my beloved. How can they ever be my enemies?"

For all his sympathy for Majnun, 'Amr could not understand this at all. What Layla's father had said about that madman finally made sense to him. And so he ordered his troops to withdraw. As swiftly as it had descended on the village, the army left—with not a word to Majnun.

Layla continued to languish in the prison of her lonely room.

Her only enjoyment was to walk in her flower garden. One day, on her way to the garden, Ibn Salam, a nobleman of wealth and power, caught a glimpse of her and fell in love at once. Without delay he sought out her father. Exhausted and disheartened by the recent battle that had left him with so many wounded, Layla's father consented to the marriage.

Layla, of course, refused her consent. She told her father, "I would be happier dead than married to that man." But all her cries and pleading fell on deaf ears. She then went to her mother, but she fared no better with her.

The wedding took place quickly. The parents were relieved that the whole ordeal was finally over. Layla, however, made it clear to her husband that she could never love him. "I will never be a wife," she declared, "so don't waste your time on me. Find yourself a mistress—I'm sure there are many who could make you happy." Despite these cold words, Ibn Salam believed that after living with him for a while, she would eventually come to her senses. He decided not to force himself on Layla, but to wait for her to come to him.

When the news of Layla's wedding reached Majnun, he wailed for days and sang songs so wrenching that all who heard them wept. His pain was so great that even the animals that gathered around him became despondent. Yet his restlessness lasted only a short while, for soon a strange inner peace seemed to settle over him. As if nothing had happened, he continued living in the ruins. Yet, not only had his feelings for Layla not changed, they had become even deeper.

It was with utmost sincerity that Majnun wrote to congratulate his beloved on her marriage: "May all the happiness in the world be yours. I ask only one thing as a token of your love—that you may remember my name, even though you have chosen another in union. Never forget that there is a man whose body, even if torn to pieces, would call only one name, and that is yours, Layla."

In answer, Layla sent an earring as a traditional sign of devotion. In her accompanying letter she said, "I cannot recall a single moment in my life that has not been spent thinking of you. I have kept my love inside for so long, without being able to tell anyone about it, while you have shouted your love to the entire world. I have been burning inside, while you have set everything around you aflame. Now I have to endure spending my life with one man when my entire soul belongs to another. Tell me, my love, which of us is more love-crazed, you or I?"

Years passed, and Majnun's parents passed away. He continued to live in the ruined building, feeling lonelier than ever. By day he wandered through the desert with his animal companions. By night be played his flute and sang his poems to the wild animals, who were now his only audience. He scratched poems to Layla in the sand with a twig. Over time, accustomed to this strange way of life, he had attained a peace and harmony that nothing could disturb.

Layla, for her part, had remained true to her love, and Ibn Salam never succeeded in getting closer to her. Although he lived with Layla, he was far apart from her. Jewelry and expensive presents had not bought her devotion, and he had given up trying to win his wife's trust. Life had become fruitless and bitter for him, and he found no tranquillity or refuge in his home. Layla and he were strangers, and he could not even share the news of the outside world with her. No words were ever heard from Layla's lips unless she were asked a question, and even then she answered as simply as possible. When, eventually, Ibn Salam succumbed to illness, he gave up the struggle, for his life offered him no hope. And so he died early one summer morning.

The death of her husband seemed to pull the plug on Layla's bottled-up emotions. People thought she was mourning Ibn Salam's death, when she was in fact crying for her long-lost love, Majnun. For years she had maintained a calm and indifferent facade, not once crying. Now she wailed long and loud over separation from her one and only.

When the traditional period of mourning was over, Layla returned to her father's house. Although still young, she had aged in spirit, reaching a maturity and wisdom rare in women her age. But while her love burned bright, Layla's health was fading, for she did not take care of herself, neglecting her meals and passing many a night without proper rest. What did she care for her body, when her only concern was Majnun? Layla herself knew well that she might not last much longer.

Finally, a chronic incurable cough that had been bothering her for a few months took its toll. As Layla lay on her deathbed, still her only thought was of Majnun. If only she could see him at least one more time! The only time she opened her eyes was to look at the door to see if her love was coming. But she knew time was running out and that she would have to go without being able to say good-bye to him. One cold autumn night, with her eyes fixed on the door, she passed quietly away, murmuring, "Majnun."

The news of Layla's death spread across the land. It was not long before it reached Majnun. When he heard the news, he swooned in the middle of the desert and remained unconscious for several days. When he came to himself, he set out at once for Layla's village. With barely enough energy to walk, he dragged his body over the sand. Thus he moved without stopping until he arrived at Layla's tomb outside the town. He mourned at her grave for days. When he found no other way to ease his pain, he gently laid his head on the grave and quietly abandoned his soul.

Majnun's body remained in Layla's tomb for a year. It was not until the anniversary of Layla's death, when her friends and relatives visited the tomb, that they found a body lying on top of the grave. A couple of school friends identified it as Majnun's. He was buried alongside Layla. The two lovers, who had been united in eternity, now were united in body as well.

It is said that sometime later, a Sufi had a dream in which Majnun appeared in the presence of the Lord. God caressed Majnun with loving-kindness and bade him sit by His side. Then he addressed Majnun: "Were you not ashamed to call Me by the name of Layla, after having drunk the wine of My Love?"

The Sufi woke up in distress. If Majnun was treated so dearly by the Lord, he wondered, what had happened to poor Layla? And as soon as he had this thought, God revealed to him the answer: "Layla's position is exalted above all, for she kept the secrets of Love concealed within."

THE GREAT SECRET OF ALEXANDER

Alexander the Great had a terrible secret that he could not entrust to anyone—no one, that is, but an old man who was his barber and confidant. The secret was that the great king had big ears! They were so big, in fact, that he had to conceal them from view for fear of ridicule. He thus covered his ears at all times with a hat. No one but the barber had any notion that he was hiding his secret under it.

In time the trusty old barber became sick and could no longer perform his duties. Reluctant as Alexander was, he had to find another man for the job. The old barber recommended Vahid, a young servant in the king's court. Vahid was honest and responsible. In fact, the barber could think of no one else fit to be trusted with the royal secret. At first the king did not want to hire another barber, but after the old man had passed away, he had no choice but to take his old servant's advice and employ Vahid. After all, the king had very long hair and could not dispense with the services of a barber.

When the time came for Vahid to cut Alexander's hair, he was so startled at the sight of the king's huge ears that he dropped the scissors. Alexander, noticing the young man's astonishment, addressed him: "If you ever tell anyone about what you just saw, I will have your tongue pulled out of the back of your mouth and then cut your head off." Vahid promised to keep the secret, but he was so frightened that all during that afternoon and for days to come, he could not think of anything but his own cut-off head, rolling on the ground.

So terrified was Vahid of the king's threat that he rarely spoke to anyone at all for fear of letting slip any hint of his terrible predicament. But in time, Vahid felt sorely in need of confiding in someone about the secret. Keeping one's own secrets is difficult enough, let alone keeping someone else's. He knew that the only way he could breathe freely again would be to tell someone about Alexander's huge ears and get it off his chest. But whom could he trust? Once word was out, it would be only a matter of days before everyone in the entire city knew about Alexander's big ears, and then Vahid's execution would follow in no time. Eventually, though, the young barber came up with an idea.

One day, Vahid left the palace secretly and headed toward a pasture not far from the city. He found a well where shepherds often stopped to rest and water their flocks. Noticing no one around, he approached the well, put his head in it, and screamed, "Alexander the Great has big ears." At once, calm and tranquillity came over him. He felt relieved and at ease, feelings he had not experienced in a long time—not since his first day as the king's barber, to be exact. Joyous with relief, he went back to the palace and was sick no more.

Months passed. Vahid seemed happy in his work, and Alexander was pleased with him. However, the king's secret was not as safe as Vahid imagined it to be. After that day in the field, a few reeds had grown out of the well. One day, a shepherd who was using the well noticed the reeds and picked one. By making a few holes in the reed, he created a musical instrument with which to amuse himself. But when he blew into it, the reed pipe produced a strange melody, in which could be heard the words, "Alexander the Great has big ears."

It so happend that Alexander himself was passing by that pasture one day when, to his astonishment, he heard the words "Alexander the Great has big ears." Following the sound of the music, he came upon the shepherd's tent and, inside, the man leisurely playing his instrument. Angry, Alexander arrested the reed player and took him back to his court without an explanation. At the palace the king grilled him about where and from whom he had heard the song. The frightened shepherd told the king about the well and the reed, and swore that he had no role in what the pipe played.

"Ridiculous!" pronounced the king upon hearing this story. And he thought to himself that the shepherd must be a friend of Vahid's, since the barber was the only soul who knew the secret. When Alexander called Vahid to the court for questioning, Vahid saw no choice but to tell the truth: "I swear to you that the only time I revealed your secret was when I shouted it into a well in the pasture."

"You shouted to a well?" asked the king, bewildered. "Why to a well?"

"Because I could no longer bear the pressure of carrying the secret within me. And since I couldn't express it to anyone, I thought a well would make the best confidant."

In order to be just, Alexander decided to have someone go to the well and pick another reed. When it was presented to him, he had the shepherd make a pipe of it. Sure enough, when Alexander took the pipe and blew in it, it sang, "Alexander the Great has big ears."

For a while, Alexander was deep in thought. Then he spoke, addressing his guards: "Let the shepherd go free." He looked at Vahid with a frown of embarrassment and said to him, "You may remain my barber if you wish."

Later, Alexander had the best calligrapher in town pen a line in gold ink. He had the writing hung in front of his bed, where he could see it the first thing every morning:

REMEMBER ALWAYS THAT YOU ARE YOUR OWN BEST
CONFIDANT; FOR EVEN A WELL, WHICH SEEMS LIKE A SAFE
PLACE, MAY BETRAY YOU.

JALALUDDIN RUMI

Persia's Greatest Mystic Poet

EVERYONE who is familiar with Eastern mysticism, particularly with Sufism, has heard of Jalaluddin Rumi, for he is one of the most celebrated and most widely translated Sufi teachers of all times. By the same token, students of poetry, especially those interested in Persian studies, look to Rumi's work as a model for the best poetry in the Persian language. Indeed, the scholars Reynold A. Nicholson and A. J. Arberry described Rumi as the greatest mystical poet of *any* age. More recently, William Chittick and Annemarie Schimmel have done valuable work in translating and interpreting Rumi's teachings. In addition, gifted poets such as Coleman Barks and Robert Bly, even though they do not read Persian, have created "versions" of Rumi that have done much to popularize his thought among English-speaking audiences.

Known by many as Maulana, "Our Master," Rumi is an outstanding figure among Sufi masters. It is said that this astonishing mystic would enter an ecstatic state of intoxication in the marketplace upon hearing the ringing of the blacksmith's hammer on the anvil. He would hear such a sound as harmonized music voicing the name of God—"Allah, Allah"—and would spontaneously whirl around, dancing to the melody he heard. The Order of the Whirling Dervishes, established by Rumi, is now known to many

Westerners through its music and dance performances in Europe and the United States.

Rumi's teachings have been valued and used by Sufi masters after him, and are studied in contemporary mystic circles. Not only Sufis, but others as well refer to his teachings for lessons, and those who enjoy poetry are intoxicated by Rumi's magical words. In the following example, translated by Nicholson, the reed symbolizes the human soul, which laments its separation from its origin (God), represented by the reed-bed:

> Listen to the reed, how it tells a tale, complaining of separations,
> Saying, "Ever since I was parted from the reed-bed, my lament
>   hath caused man and woman to moan.
> I want a bosom torn by severance, that I may unfold the pain of
>   love-desire.
> Everyone who is left far from his source wishes back the time
>   when he was united with it.
> In every company I uttered my wailful notes; I consorted with the
>   unhappy and with them who rejoice.
> Everyone became my friend from his own opinion; none sought
>   out my secrets from within me.
> My secret is not far from my plaint, but ear and eye lack the light
>   (whereby it should be apprehended).
> Body is not veiled from soul, nor soul from body, yet none is
>   permitted to see the soul."[1]

RUMI'S LIFE AND TEACHINGS

Since Rumi lived most of his life in Konya, a city in present-day Turkey, the Turks claim him as being Turkish. The Afghans raise another claim, arguing that since this great master was born in Balkh, a city now located in Afghanistan, he must be considered of Afghani origin. Yet most scholars agree that Rumi is Persian. The reason for this is twofold: Balkh, the city in which Rumi was born, was a Persian city at the time of his birth, and all of Rumi's books were written in the Persian language. However, Rumi did choose Konya as his place of residence and remained there until his death. Of course, in a sense, place of birth and nationality are of little importance, for the true mystic is universal in spirit.

Jalaluddin Rumi was born on September 30, 1207. His father, Baha'uddin Walad, was a well-known and respected preacher, jurisprudent, and Sufi, whose spiritual lineage was traced to Ahmad al-Ghazzali, a famous Sufi master of an earlier century. Baha Walad was an authority in both exoteric and esoteric Islam. As an exoteric authority, he taught Islamic law (Shari'a) in mosques and other public places; as an esoteric teacher, he met in more private environments with those who sought his teachings.

Although Baha married a member of the royal family, he was opposed to the policies of the ruler, Kharazmshah. The king attended most of Baha's exoteric lessons, but eventually grew jealous of his popularity and suspicious of his teachings, which brought controversy to the kingdom. Thus, when the Mongols invaded Balkh in 1219, Baha with his family left the city that had become so inhospitable to him, to make the pilgrimage to Mecca. No doubt he was aware that they would never see Balkh again.

On their way, they stopped in Nishapur, the hometown of the great Attar, who was by then an old man. Attar accepted the guests warmly — including young Jalal, whose potential greatness he apparently recognized, as seen in this description by Ira Friedlander: "Baha and Attar sat together, drank the customary tea, and spoke of passages in the Koran. Several hours later, the travelers were preparing to depart. As young Jalal walked closely behind his father, Attar turned to one of the dervishes and remarked, 'Look at this peculiar situation; there goes a sea followed by an ocean.' "[2]

During that visit, Attar presented Jalal with his *Book of Secrets,* telling Baha, "Your son will soon be kindling fire in all the world's lovers of God." Attar's writings, teaching the principles of Sufism through stories and fables, would become one of the major influences on Rumi's work.

After the pilgrimage, Baha and his family set out for Asia Minor. On a stop in the city of Larnada, Jalal, then twenty-one years old, married Gawhar, the daughter of one of Baha's friends. The Seljuk king, 'Ala'uddin Kayqobad, who was ruling in the nearby city of Konya, became aware of Baha's new place of residence. (Konya was later taken over by the Ottoman Empire.) The king, who respected science and philosophy and promoted scholarly works, wrote to Baha, offering him a place of residence and an official position at the *madrasa* (university) at Konya. Upon Baha's acceptance, the king received him and his family warmly. Baha took up residence in Konya and stayed there for the next several years. Since Konya (the ancient Iconium) was also called Rum, Jalal adopted the name Rumi as his nom de plume.

Having learned at his father's knee since childhood, Rumi had by this time mastered Arabic grammar, prosody, the Qur'an, jurisprudence, Hadith (the traditions of the Prophet's sayings and deeds), Qur'anic commentary, history, dogmatics, theology, logic, philosophy, mathematics, and astronomy. When his father died in 1231, Rumi, at the age of twenty-four, succeeded to his father's position as teacher.

Rumi is assumed to have become familiar with the principles of Sufism under his father's guidance, although Sufi scholars believe that he did not begin formal Sufi training until 1232, when a high-ranking student of his father's, Burhanuddin Tirmidhi, came to Konya in hopes of visiting his master. Upon learning of Baha's death, Tirmidhi took on the task of teaching Jalal the principles of the Path. The two traveled to Aleppo and Damascus, where Rumi came into contact with one of the most influential Sufi masters of all times, Ibn 'Arabi of Spain. Tirmidhi continued to impart the disciplines of Sufism to Rumi until his death in 1240.

Rumi remained in his conventional post at the university even though he had become an accomplished Sufi master. In the words of William Chittick, he "had traversed the stations of the Sufi path and realized the direct and immediate vision of God he discusses so constantly in his verses. But, in spite of his spiritual attainments, Rumi's outward life remained the same as it had always been. He assumed the customary activities and trappings of a staid and honored doctor of the law. Sometimes, he would discuss the spiritual mysteries in his sermons, but he never gave any outward indication that he was any different than other jurisprudents and lawyers for having knowledge of them."[3]

Rumi gained widespread respect and fame as an ordinary professor, and people from all parts of the East came to him for advice and lectures. Probably he would have remained so, if it were not for his encounter with a remarkable spiritual personality, Shamsuddin Tabrizi.

The mysterious Shams first met Rumi in 1244, when Rumi was thirty-eight—an event that changed Rumi's life forever. Had Rumi not met Shams, he might not have written poems at all—and, in fact, Rumi as we know him today might not have existed. As Chittick puts it, Shams's influence " 'exteriorized' Rumi's inner contemplative states in the form of poetry and set the ocean of his being into a motion which resulted in vast waves that transformed the history of Persian literature."[4] Shams disappeared after three years, leaving no trace. According to Idries Shah, some Sufis (including Rumi's son, Sultan Walad) "equated Shams with the mysterious Khidr, the guide and patron of Sufis, who appears and then passes out of normal cognition after transmitting his message."[5]

Without doubt, the relationship between Rumi and Shams is one of the most extraordinary of spiritual bonds known to history. Not very often is Divine Love manifested externally in a relationship between two humans.[6] As a perfect master, Shams brought out the latent perfection within Rumi. It is important, therefore, to learn something of the life of Shams in order to better under-stand his role in the transformation of Rumi.

SHAMSUDDIN, THE "SUN OF RELIGION"

For the most part, Shams remains a mysterious figure. Of his teachings, nothing remains but one book, *The Articles of Shams Tabrizi*. It consists of a series of talks Shams gave at Sufi gatherings in Konya. Apparently Shams did not write down his thoughts. Much of what has remained of his teachings is known through the re-corded observations of Sultan Walad, Rumi's son. There are many poems and tales about Shams, and yet his family background and personal history are for the most part unknown. However, some speculations about his life have been made, based on the available sources.

It has been suggested that Muhammad Malekdad, later given the title Shamsuddin ("Sun of Religion") Tabrizi, was born in the city of Tabriz in Persia in 1148 C.E. In his childhood he showed excep-tional traits. Instead of playing, he would attend religious lectures and study the Sufi masters of the past. At an early age he experi-enced a feeling of yearning, a seeking within himself for a beloved. Since he found no children of his age who understood him, he spent most of his time alone. For this reason, Shams always seemed to be sad.

Shams's parents thought that perhaps his languor was due to a typical youthful wish for something he could not have. On this subject, Shams later said, "They asked me, 'Why are you de-pressed? Do you want clothes of silver and gold?' I answered, 'No, I wish someone would take away what I already am wearing.' "[7] By this, Shams meant that he wished for the garment of egotism to be removed from his soul. What an extraordinary idea for a child to express! Anyone who heard such answers from him could not comprehend the deeper meanings behind his words and must have assumed him to be unbalanced—unless the listener happened to be a highly developed Sufi initiate.

It is related that one day a Sufi was passing by a teahouse, where Shams—who was a young boy at the time—and his father were having some tea. The father, who had his back turned toward Shams, was busy talking to his friends. Upon observing this, the Sufi made a fist and angrily exclaimed, "If it were not for my respect for your child, I would punish you for your impudence toward him." He then bowed chivalrously to Shams and, as was the Sufi custom, said in parting, "May your time be happy." This phrase, which can be taken as a pleasantry like "Have a nice day," actually has deeper significance, since here "time" in Sufi symbolism refers to union with God.

In his teenage years, Shams went through a period of insomnia and loss of appetite that lasted longer than a month. When asked why he was not eating or sleeping, he answered, "Why should I eat or sleep, when God, Who created me this way, is not speaking to me directly? What need have I to eat or sleep? If He talks to me, and I find out why I was created, whence I came, and whither I am going, then I will eat and sleep." Later, Shams talked about this period as a time of True Love, when his passion for the Divine made him indifferent to normal physical needs.

When Shams reached adulthood, a Sufi teacher, Abu Bakr Silah-Baf, started to train him in the stages of the spiritual path, but it was not long before the master realized that Shams had reached such a high level that it was no longer necessary for him to remain a student. Upon his master's suggestion, Shams started to search for a student of his own, one who would live up to his expectations. This search lasted most of his life. From city to city and country to country Shams traveled. He took any job, from teaching school to unskilled labor, and never accepted any pay for his services nor had any more money than was necessary. He gave the appearance of a beggar in his coarse, patched black cloak.

On a stop in Baghdad, Shams met with Auhaduddin Kermani, a Sufi shaykh who believed that the only way to reach a high level of spirituality is by observing the divine attributes in the beauties of Creation. Their meeting is described in the following story.

> Shams asked the shaykh, "What are you doing?"
>
> "I am looking at the moon's reflection in this lake," replied the shaykh.
>
> "Unless you suffer from a boil on your neck, why not look at the sky? Are you so blind that you do not see the true object in all you contemplate?"
>
> Shams's reply had such an effect on the shaykh that he asked Shams to accept him as his disciple.
>
> "You do not have the strength to bear my company," replied Shams.
>
> "The strength is within me," said the shaykh. "Please accept me."
>
> "Then bring me a pitcher of wine, and we will drink together in the Baghdad market."
>
> Fearing public opinion (because alcohol is forbidden by Islam), the shaykh replied, "I cannot do this."
>
> Shams shouted, "You are too timid for me. You haven't the strength to be among the intimate friends of God. I seek only him who knows how to reach the Truth."

Shams took no heed of public opinion or the clergy in his actions, which were motivated purely by the love of God.

Shams continued traveling from place to place in search of an ideal student until finally, one cold morning in November 1244, when he was in his sixties, he arrived in Konya and met Jalaluddin Rumi.

SHAMS AND RUMI

Like two lightning bolts striking each other, Rumi and Shams, when they met, created one of the most unforgettable storms in the history of the spiritual world. Many different versions of this meeting have been told. Following are the two that are most often cited.

One day Rumi was riding on horseback, with a crowd of his students and laypeople following him. He stopped at the university where he was to give his regular class. A wretched-looking figure followed Rumi into the classroom. It was Shamsuddin Tabrizi. Without asking for permission to enter or speak up, Shams asked, "Who was greater—Bayazid Bastami or Prophet Muhammad?"

Rumi, who felt the energy of Shams's glance piercing his soul, replied, "Prophet Muhammad was greater."

Shams said, "Did not the Prophet say, 'We have not known Thee as Thou deservest to be known,' whereas Bayazid exclaimed, 'How great is my station; glory be upon me who is exalted, whose dignity is upraised'?" Shams, seeing that Rumi was unable to answer this question, pointed out that Bayazid's thirst for the Divine was quenched after drinking a mouthful, whereas the Prophet's thirst was never quenched, for he was always thirsty for more water of divine knowledge.

Finding himself weakened by Shams's powerful words, Rumi fell to the ground at Shams's feet, crying until he lost consciousness. When Rumi came to, his head was on the lap of Shams, who was seated. Shortly afterward, the two men went into seclusion together for three months.

Another version describes a different event, but one of the same magnitude:

One day Rumi was sitting in his personal library, with a group of his students gathered around him for his lecture. Suddenly, Shams Tabrizi entered uninvited. He uttered a greeting and sat down. Then he pointed to the books that were stacked in a corner and asked Rumi, "What are these?"

Rumi, who had judged Shams from his appearance to be a beggar, answered, "You would not understand." He had not even finished his sentence when flames of fire started to rise from the books in the corner. Frightened, Rumi cried out, "What is this?"

Shams replied calmly, "Nor would you understand this." So saying, he left the room. Rumi cried out again and ran after Shams. Thus, he abandoned his teaching post and entered a period of retreat with Shams.

Whichever account we accept, one thing is certain: Rumi beheld in Shams's very being the burning fire of love. Rumi, who thought himself a master of all existing knowledge and science, found himself clinging to his master Shams. He left all that he had for the love of the Eternal Beloved, Who was now personified in Shams. He quit tutoring, lecturing at the university, and his other daily activities. He knelt before the teacher and, despite all his advanced degrees, began from the beginning, learning the ABCs of Divine Love.

Shams and Rumi spent three or four months in a retreat cell. No one knows what Shams taught Rumi in that period. What contemporary observers saw was that Rumi emerged from the retreat at the age of thirty-eight a changed man. Instead of giving religious lectures and holding group prayers, he would lead Sufi sama' and whirling dances.[8] Instead of engaging in philosophical discussions, he would listen to the music of the reed pipe or play the rabab, a string instrument. He who had no background in poetry began to compose glorious verses expressing his love of God. The fire lighted by Shams had transformed Rumi.

According to Chittick, "One could say that without Shams, there would have been no Rumi. Nevertheless, one must not overestimate the role Shams played, since Rumi was already an accomplished adept when Shams arrived on the scene."[9] Shams himself confessed, "If I worked hard for one hundred years, I would not be able to acquire one-tenth of the knowledge Rumi has. But out of his extreme humility, Rumi considers his knowledge as nonexistent. Like a two-year-old child who listens to his father with love, and like a new Moslem who knows nothing of the faith, this man listens to me. I am embarrassed by this."[10]

This love of Rumi for his teacher did not go unreciprocated. Shams found the Divine in the face of Rumi as well. His search had come to an end when he met this exceptional lover of God. He said, "I wanted someone after my own heart, someone to turn to, for I had become tired of myself. Now I have found the one who would understand what I say."[11]

Since Rumi was spending much of his time with Shams and had quit teaching, his students felt jealous of Shams and missed the company of their teacher. As a result, they conspired against Shams. Thus, after a sixteen-month residence in Konya, Shams left for Damascus. Rumi, who could not endure the separation from Shams, sent his son, Sultan Walad, after him. Shams agreed to come back to Konya; however, not long after his return, in 1247, he vanished mysteriously, and no further information has ever been found about him, even to this day. Some researchers report that he was murdered by Rumi's jealous students and that the body was destroyed afterward.

LIFE AFTER SHAMS

After Shams's disappearance, Rumi felt a great longing and began to write his many love poems, using Shams as the subject. Chittick writes, "In these verses, as in all of Rumi's poetry, it quickly becomes clear that the outward form is but a veil over the inward meaning. Separation from Shams al-Din, the 'Sun of Religion,' was but the appearance; separation from the Divine Beloved, 'the Sun of the Sun,' was the reality."[12] These poems typically reflect the spiritual station of Rumi; some allude to the experiences of Union. Although it was (and is) customary for poets to include their own name in the last line of a ghazal, as a form of artistic signature, the majority of Rumi's ghazals end with the name of Shams—perhaps

as a gesture of humility, or out of respect for the role Shams played
in Rumi's life.

When Rumi realized that Shams would not return, he dressed
in mourning—an Indian cloak and a woolen hat. Then he hosted
regular *sama'* gatherings in memory of Shams. It was at these *sama'*
sessions that the Mevlevi Order, the Order of Whirling Dervishes,
began to take shape.

Most scholars agree that the whirling dance was taught to Rumi
by Shams. It is said that this dance is symbolic of the circular
motion of the soul, which takes place because of the Sufi's love for
and complete attention to God. In fact, the *sama'* of the Mevlevi
dervishes, according to Annemarie Schimmel, is "an expression of
the sweetest and deepest secrets of mystical love. The dervishes,
after slowly walking around the room thrice, each time kissing the
Pir's (Master's) hand, suddenly throw off their black gowns (their
earthly bodies, as it were) and emerge in their white gowns of
eternal light, spinning around their axes as well as whirling around
the center, as though the atoms were dancing around the sun
which attracts them to set them in motion—heavenly dance, dance
of immortality, as Mawlana [Rumi] had described it in ever so many
of his verses."[13] This tradition has continued for six hundred years.

From 1247 to the end of his life in 1273, Rumi composed a vast
output of verse. Unpremeditated and unrevised, his spontaneous
poetry takes advantage of rhyme and rhythm to produce an in-
credible melody when recited out loud. Combined with instru-
mental music, it has the effect of seeming to penetrate the soul of
the listener. Rumi's poems contain all of his teachings. Yet he apparently did not acknowledge himself as a poet. His humility is
evident in a famous remark of his: "I am affectionate to such a
degree that when these friends come to me, for fear that they may
be wearied, I speak poetry so that they may be occupied with that.
Otherwise, what have I to do with poetry? By Allah, I care nothing
for poetry, and there is nothing worse in my eyes than that. It has

become incumbent upon me, as when a man plunges his hands into tripe and washes it out for the sake of a guest's appetite, because the guest's appetite is for tripe."[14]

More than seventy of Rumi's poems were dedicated to his companion Salahuddin Zarkub, who happened to be the father-in-law of Rumi's son, Sultan Walad. An uneducated and simple-hearted man, Zarkub was a good friend to Rumi for ten years, until 1259, when Zarkub passed away. Thereafter Husamuddin Chelabi, one of Rumi's disciples, became his master's close companion for the rest of his life. It was Husam who gave Rumi the idea of writing his most important work, the *Mathnawi-yi ma'nawi*.

Apparently, Husam noticed that Rumi's disciples regularly read the poetry of San'ai and Attar in their gatherings. These poets were the first Sufi masters to teach in the language of poetry. Their verse contained interesting stories carrying important Sufi messages. One day Husam suggested to Rumi that he write in the same style as San'ai and Attar, both to meet his disciples' need to learn and to complement his other literary productions. Upon hearing this request, Rumi at once drew a piece of paper from his turban and wrote the first poem of the *Mathnawi*. After that, the two met every day. Rumi dictated the poems to Husam, who wrote them down and, at the end of each session, read the notes back to Rumi for corrections or additions. This work began sometime in 1260 and continued, with intermittent delays, until the death of Rumi in 1273, where the work breaks off in the middle of a story.

Sultan Walad guided the aspirants of the Mevlevi Order after the death of his father, and Husamuddin Chelabi succeeded Sultan upon his death. Throughout history, the descendants or elevated disciples of Rumi have taken the responsibility of guiding the Mevlevi dervishes. Today, as has been their tradition for over six hundred years, they have their center in Konya, where Rumi lies buried.

RUMI'S WORKS

The *Mathnawi*, known as the Persian Qur'an, consists of rhyming couplets that make up six books of poetry—a total of more than 25,700 lines of verse. Nicholson describes this epic work as containing almost as many verses as the *Iliad* and *Odyssey* put together and about twice as many as the *Divine Comedy*—"and these comparisons make it appear shorter than it actually is."[15]

The *Mathnawi* can also be considered a collection of fables, tales, and jokes that Rumi took from the Qur'an, from the Hadith, and simply from day-to-day events and problems. Most of the stories are long, and, owing to the poet's habit of planting moral advice in the middle, their flow is sometimes temporarily lost, only to resume many pages further on. In this chapter we retell a few stories from this important collection.

The only other poetic work of Rumi's is the *Divan-i Shams-i Tabriz* (The Divan of Shams of Tabriz), which contains 35,000 lines of verse. It was written over a period of thirty years, from the time of Shams's disappearance until Rumi's death. This work consists of the *ghazals* that Rumi wrote after he was separated from Shams. Compared with the *Mathnawi*, which is a more sober work, the *Divan* more clearly represents a sense of the intoxication of the mystical state. It is obvious that many of the poems were written after Rumi had been experiencing the ecstasy of *sama'* while whirling or during meditation. The poems reveal some secrets of the Sufi experience. In addition to praising Shams, Rumi makes reference in the *Divan* to Salahuddin Zarkub and Husamuddin Chelabi. For Rumi, these three men are reflections of the Divine, and their companionship imparts a sense of Union.

Apparently Rumi also composed some poems in Turkish. However, they have not been collected into one volume.

Fihi ma fihi (In It Is What's in It) is a prose collection of Rumi's talks to his disciples. It is similar to the *Mathnawi* in that it discusses

Sufi teachings by means of comparisons and examples. *Majalis-i Sab'a* (Seven Sessions), also a prose work, is a collection of Rumi's lectures. These talks were given to the public (not necessarily Sufis) before his meeting with Shams. The last of his works is the *Makatib* (Letters), 145 of Rumi's letters to friends, disciples, and family members. A good number of them are letters of recommendation to princes and noblemen on behalf of a friend or student. In general, these letters have only historical significance.

THE KING AND THE HANDMAIDEN

Once upon a time, there lived a king in a beautiful land. One day, on his way to the palace in his coach, the king saw a handmaiden sitting by the road. The pretty slave girl stole his heart, and the king desired to have her. So he sent a servant to recompense her master and then brought her to his palace.

As the days passed, the poor maiden in captivity became sick, lost weight, and grew paler every day. Every time the king went to see her, she refused him. And so the king sent for the royal physicians, who were the best doctors in all the land, offering valuable gifts and rewards to whoever could cure the girl—but to no avail. Not one of them could diagnose the illness, let alone prescribe an effective treatment.

Deeply discouraged and worried about his beloved, the king ran to the temple to pray. He wailed for hours, imploring God from the depths of his heart to cure his beloved. Finally, exhausted from weeping, he fell asleep. The Lord, Who had heard his prayers, spoke to him in a dream: "Tomorrow a Divine Physician will come to your town. He has the cure for the girl."

The next morning, the king went with his companions to the gates of the city to await the Doctor. In the distance they spied a man approaching. When he drew closer and the king saw his face, his body began shaking. The radiant presence of the Doctor had taken over his soul, and he began to cry, saying, "I realize now that I have been seeking You, not the girl. She was but an excuse, and the cause of my awakening now."

The Doctor was brought to the palace, and he asked to be alone with the maiden. After talking gently to the girl and reassuring her that her secrets would be safe with him, the Doctor asked about her past. While he felt her pulse, the girl told him where she was from and what her duties had been before the king bought her. There was no change in her pulse. Then the Doctor asked about the places to which she had traveled. When he asked about Samarkand, her pulse beat faster. He asked more about that city and about the people she had met there. Finally, her pulse still beating rapidly, the girl mentioned a certain goldsmith for whom she had worked for a couple of years. The Doctor had discovered her illness.

"Her problem is of heart, not of the body," he pronounced to the king. "To cure this girl, you must follow my instructions." The king said that he would obey the Doctor wholeheartedly. So the goldsmith was sent for with an offer of money and property on the king's land. Tempted by the windfall, the goldsmith left his family, home, and work immediately and moved to the new town.

With the king's blessing, the handsome young man was married to the beautiful maiden, and they took up residence in the royal palace. The couple enjoyed their new life together for six months, by which time the girl had fully recovered from her illness. At that point, the Doctor ordered a potion made for the goldsmith to drink every morning. The concoction made him pale and weak, and he became so ugly that his wife eventually fell out of love with him. Finally, one day, the goldsmith, who had not gotten out of bed for months, died, and the girl became free of his bond.

What lesson can we draw from this strange story? Obviously, that any love which arises for the sake of outward beauty is not true love: in the end it is but a disgrace. Yet this moral that worldly love is transient is not the only message to be found in Rumi's tale. The deeper meaning, addressed to the Sufis, may be gleaned from the following key to symbology:

King	=	Spirit
Companions of the king	=	Love
Handmaiden	=	Heart
Royal physicians	=	Intellect
Divine Physician	=	Sufi Master
Goldsmith	=	Ego
Potion	=	Mortification

The human Spirit, with its companion, Love, descends from the higher world to bring the Heart towards the Unity. The purpose of the Spirit is to encompass the Heart, to rid it of material desires so that it can bear God's secrets. However, it finds the Heart trapped by Ego. By creating desires and wants, the Ego has taken complete possession of the Heart. Heart is pulled one way by the Spirit and the opposite way by the egotistical desires. Since the Heart cannot choose between the two, an imbalance is created, and the body becomes sick.

Intellect tries curing the Heart by treating the body. However, since the treatment has to be for the Heart, not the body, Intellect's efforts are useless. Therefore, the Spirit turns to its Divine Source for help. The Compassionate One sends the Master, in the form of a Doctor, to help Spirit. The Divine Physician, who knows that the disease of the Heart is the result of this imbalance, immediately realizes that the problem lies within the Ego.

Now, it is often true that a physician trained in diseases of the body is unable to treat a patient who has psychological problems. However, a Master—who is a doctor of the Spirit—can diagnose and cure such an imbalance.

After the Master discovers the problems that Ego has created for the Heart, he decides to bring Ego face to face with the Heart. Thus, Heart meets with the complexes, the clusters of worldly impressions, desires, and attachments that make up the Ego. As a result, desires are fulfilled and the illness disappears.

Now comes the time for transformation. To accomplish this, the Master, with the help of mortification, weakens the Ego. Eventually Heart, which was trapped in the tempting illusions of Ego's desires, finds itself no longer interested in such superficiality. Finally, in fulfillment of Spirit's aim of redeeming the Heart, the Heart is released from the bonds of egotism. Thus, the Heart, now free, can serve her king, the Spirit, and begin to learn the secrets of God.

THE GROCER AND HIS PARROT

A grocer found a beautiful parrot for sale in the market, and, excited about his purchase, set about installing a hook in the ceiling of his little shop's ceiling, from which he intended to hang the parrot's cage. He had found the perfect location, too — right in the doorway, where the magnificent bird would be easily visible from the outside. The grocer figured that the parrot, with its colorful plumage and its gift of speech, would attract many customers. The bird would thus be a good investment, boosting business for the shop, which admittedly had not been doing so well lately.

And sure enough, it was just as the grocer had hoped. As soon as the parrot opened his mouth, curious passersby who heard him from outside would enter into the store to listen to the bird's interesting chatter, and would end up buying something out of courtesy. The shopkeeper named the parrot Sweet Tongue. Not only was the bird the star of the marketplace, but eventually he also became a good friend of the grocer himself.

Sweet Tongue was not an ordinary parrot. He seemed not merely to mimic words but actually to understand their meaning.

He could hold conversations with his grocer friend and, interestingly enough, listened to the man's daily complaints and offered advice. And despite his name, Sweet Tongue would say anything he liked, whether it was something nice or not. This sort of talk, even if it was a harsh criticism of the human listener, was not offensive to those who were so addressed. As a matter of fact, people accepted the bird's comments in good humor.

The business of the grocery flourished, enabling the grocer to move into a bigger store and expand his inventory. Business was improving so greatly that he added a few displays of herbal medicine to the store. Eventually, after the grocer had invested a large sum of money in the shop, he decided to make a large part of it a complete apothecary. Hundreds of bottles, large and small, containing all sorts of oils and ointments, potions and syrups, went on display.

The appreciative grocer became very fond of his feathered companion and rewarded the bird by letting him fly freely about the store. One morning, as the grocer was unlocking the door to his shop, he smelled a strong aroma coming from inside. Once the door was open, he saw Sweet Tongue flying from one corner to the other; all the bottles had been broken and were scattered on the floor. Apparently, the parrot had hit the bottles while flying and had knocked them over. It is no exaggeration to say that the new apothecary displays were utterly in ruins. A great investment seemed to have gone down the drain.

At first the grocer was in shock. But as the minutes went by and he regained his senses, he became enraged. He seized Sweet Tongue by the throat and hit him on the head so many times that the poor bird almost expired on the spot. Then he threw the bird into his cage and sat down and cried over the misfortune. Hours later, the grocer realized that because he had struck the parrot's head, Sweet Tongue had lost his head feathers. The poor parrot, now totally bald, was confined to his cage once again.

In time, the grocer was able to recover the losses to his business. However, there was one piece of irreparable damage: Sweet Tongue, who now looked rather ugly, had fallen silent after the incident. Naturally the customers who came merely to enjoy Sweet Tongue's chatter and bright appearance stopped shopping at the store. The grocer's business, which had flourished before, began to decline.

The grocer planned various schemes to make the parrot talk again. He tried tempting him with delicious nuts, but the bird showed no interest in such food. Then he brought a musician to the store to play. The music was intended to revive Sweet Tongue's spirit, so that he would forgive the grocer and speak again. But still he remained mute. In a last attempt, the grocer brought a female parrot and put her cage in front of Sweet Tongue's. The grocer told Sweet Tongue that he would set both of them free to fly about the store if only he would talk. However, the bird ignored both the grocer and the female parrot. When the grocer opened the door of the cage and encouraged Sweet Tongue to fly around the shop, the bird squeezed into the back corner of his cage and refused to budge.

Finally, the grocer gave up trying. Resigned to the idea that the parrot had gone dumb after the shock to his body, he left Sweet Tongue in peace. Yet, not totally without hope, the grocer gave alms and said prayers. Perhaps through his piety the parrot would eventually talk again.

One day, a wandering dervish with patched cloak and beggar's bowl was passing by the store. He was totally bald. Suddenly, a nasal voice from inside the store called out, "Hey, you! How did you end up bald? Did you break some bottles, too?"

The bald dervish turned around to see who had addressed him. To his surprise he saw that it was a parrot speaking to him. The grocer, elated by this sudden stroke of fortune, invited the dervish in and explained the story of the medicine bottles and how the parrot had become bald and speechless. The dervish approached the cage and said to Sweet Tongue, "So, you think the reason I am bald is because of a situation similar to yours?"

"What else could it be?" replied the parrot.

The dervish smiled. "My friend, let me give you a word of advice: no two leaves on a tree are the same! Neither are two persons with similar appearances alike, for one person may reflect on his life's experiences while the other remains ignorant. There are many, though, who think that, in fact, the two are alike. How oblivious they are, for there is no disparity greater than that between the wise and the ignorant. It is like the difference between Moses' staff and Aaron's—one has the power of God, the other that of man; one makes miracles, the other magic. Nothing causes more trouble than the human habit of judging things by their appearance, because what might look the same on the surface may not be the same in essence. Take the example of the honeybee and the bumblebee: they look alike, but from one comes honey, while from the other comes pain."

The dervish stopped talking and gave the grocer an insightful look, as if reading his soul. The parrot was now sitting quietly in his cage, and the grocer seemed stunned. The dervish then smiled and, without a word, walked out.

Moments later, when the grocer came to his sense, he realized that such a lesson as he had been given was not to be taken lightly. He ran outside to thank the Sufi. But the man had disappeared, and no one could recall having seen a bald dervish in the bazaar that day.

THE PHILOSOPHER AND THE SKIPPER

'Ali was a philosopher who thought he knew all there was to know. Everyone agreed that he had a broad knowledge of the sciences and the arts, yet he insisted on bragging to one and all that he was the smartest man in town.

'Ali's friend Sam* was bothered by this arrogance and tried hard to make 'Ali see the world around him with open eyes. His arguments, however, were unproductive. After talking the matter over with a sailor he knew, Sam decided to encourage 'Ali to go on a sea voyage. Such a trip would show 'Ali other ways of life and expose him to difficulties that he would otherwise not experience. To his surprise, 'Ali liked the idea, and so the arrangements were made.

Once at sea, 'Ali talked philosophy with the sailors. The skipper listened patiently for a while without saying a word, but finally he interrupted to complain that he was bored by this talk.

"Do you know anything about philosophy?" 'Ali asked.

"I'm afraid not," the skipper replied.

"What a shame," said 'Ali, shaking his head, "for half of your life has been wasted, not having such knowledge." The skipper let that comment go unanswered and kept busy steering the ship.

They sailed for days. 'Ali was enjoying himself, talking most of the time. He was so busy explaining his ideas on how governments should run their countries and how leaders should address different problems that he did not bother to learn anything about sailing. Even when they cast anchor alongside a small island for a change of pace, 'Ali, who didn't know how to swim, did not take advantage of the calm waters to ask his sailor friends for swimming lessons. Neither did he care to ask any questions about their life at sea.

The next night, while they were in midocean, heading back home, the captain started to get worried. There were unmistakable signs that a storm was on the way. The crew prepared to face the emergency. Only 'Ali remained calm in his cabin, his mind occupied with loftier matters.

*Pronounced Sām, with a long *a* as in *father*.

The wind blew hard, wresting control of the ship from the captain's hands. The sailors, panicking, were thrown from side to side as the vessel pitched in the swells. There was so much water on deck from the heavy rain and giant waves that the ship was riding noticeably low in the water. The skipper shouted for the crew to prepare to abandon ship.

The ship's only lifeboat was lowered into the water, and soon it became obvious that it would not hold all the men. The skipper and several sailors were preparing to jump into the open sea and take their chances swimming. It was then that the skipper remembered 'Ali. He asked one of the sailors to find him.

'Ali was holding on to his cabin door, trying to maintain his balance. The sailor screamed at him, "Hurry up, we must abandon the ship. It is sinking!" 'Ali, confused, was helped to the deck.

The skipper hollered, "Do you know how to swim?"

"No!" 'Ali shouted back.

The skipper shook his head. "What a shame, for all of your life has been wasted, not having such knowledge."

The skipper and his crew were saved that night by another vessel after the storm subsided. Even 'Ali was rescued, with the help of a couple of sailors who kept him afloat. From that day on, not a peep was heard from 'Ali about his vast knowledge of philosophy.

A few years after the incident, 'Ali presented a gift to the skipper, who was now a close friend of his. It was a framed painting of a ship in a stormy sea. A couplet was inscribed beneath the picture:

Only empty objects remain on top of the water.
Become empty of human attributes, and you will float on the
    ocean of creation.

MUSA AND THE SHEPHERD

There was once a free-spirited shepherd who possessed neither money nor the desire for it. All he had was a pure and kind heart, a heart that beat with the love of his Lord. All day long he wandered with his flock through pastures, plains, and fields, singing and talking all the while to his Beloved God: "O dear Lord, where are You to Whom I dedicate my life? Where are You for Whom I am but a servant? O God, for Whom I live and breathe, by Whose grace I exist, I would sacrifice my sheep for the sight of You. . . ."

One day Musa—the prophet Moses—was passing by a pasture on his way to the city. He noticed the shepherd, who was sitting by his flock with his face tilted up to the sky, addressing God: "Where are You so that I may sew Your clothes, mend Your socks, and make Your bed? Where are You so that I may comb Your hair and kiss Your feet? Where are You so that I may polish Your shoes and bring You milk to drink?"

Musa approached the shepherd and asked him, "Whom are you talking to?"

"To the One who has created us. The One who is Lord over day and night, earth and sky."

Musa became enraged with the shepherd's reply. "How dare you talk to God like that! What you are saying is blasphemous. You should stuff cotton in your mouth if you cannot control your tongue. Then, at least, no one would hear your outrageous, insulting words, which have poisoned the very atmosphere. You must stop speaking like that at once, lest the Almighty punish the entire human race for your sin!"

The shepherd, who had arisen upon recognizing the prophet, stood shaken. With tears running down his cheek, he listened as Musa continued: "Is the Almighty God a mere human being that

He should wear shoes and socks? Is He an unformed infant in need
of milk to make Him grow? Of course not! God is complete in
Himself, needless of all. By speaking with the Lord as you have
done, you disgrace not only yourself but all the rest of God's creatures. You are naught but a defier of religion and an enemy of God!
Go and ask for forgiveness, if you have any sense left!"

The simple shepherd did not really understand what he had said
to God that was so rude, or why the prophet had called him an
enemy. Yet he knew that a prophet of God must know better than
anyone else. Barely able to contain his sobs, he told Musa, "You
have set fire to my soul. From now on my mouth is sealed!" With
a deep sigh, he turned away from his flock and walked toward the
desert.

Feeling proud that he had corrected a wayward soul, Musa was
continuing on his way toward the city when the Almighty addressed him: "Why did you come between Us and Our loyal servant? Why did you separate the lover from the Beloved? We have
sent you so that you could unite one to the other, not break their
ties." Musa listened to the Heavenly Words in awe and humility.

"We did not create this world in order to profit from it; Creation is for the benefit of the creatures. We have no need of praise
or worship; it is the worshipers who benefit from it. Remember
that in Love, words are only the outer husk and mean nothing. We
pay no heed to the beauty of the phrase or the composition of the
sentence. We look only at the inner condition of the heart. In that
way We know the sincerity of Our creatures, even though their
words may be artless. For those who burn with Love have burned
their words as well."

The Voice from Heaven continued: "Those who are bound by
propriety are not like those who are bound in Love, and the nation
of religion is not the nation of Love, for the lover knows no other
religion than the Beloved Himself."

The Lord thus taught Musa the secrets of Love, and now that

he understood his mistake, the prophet regretted his outburst. And so he hurried off to find the shepherd and apologize.

For days Musa wandered over grassland and desert, asking people if they had seen the shepherd. Each one pointed in a different direction. It seemed a hopeless quest, but finally Musa came upon the shepherd sitting by a spring, his clothes torn and disheveled. He was in a state of deep meditation and did not notice Musa, who waited a long while. At last the shepherd lifted his head and looked at the prophet.

"I have an important message for you," said Musa. "God has spoken, and He told me that there is no need for etiquette in your speech to God. You are free to talk to him in any way you like, with any words you may choose. For what I thought was your blasphemy is actually the faith and love that saves the world."

The shepherd answered simply: "I have passed the stage of words and phrases. My heart is now illuminated with His presence. I cannot explain my state to you. Nor can words describe it for others." He then rose and started on his way.

Musa watched the departing figure of the shepherd until he could see it no more. Then he set out on the road to the nearest city, marveling at the lesson he had received from a simple, unlettered worshiper.

'ABDUL-RAHMAN JAMI

The Last of the Great Storytellers

I am like a ball in the field of months and years.
In fate's game of polo, I roll from station to station.

In the year eight hundred and seventeen from the Prophet's
        journey,
    who left Mecca for Yathreb and built his camp of majesty,
From the top of the majestic mountain of pre-eternity,
I opened my wings and flew to this low valley of futility.

Today I have dragged to the year eight hundred and ninety-three
the ruins of the chariot of life in this narrow passage of fantasy.

In between these two dates, in my lifetime,
Oh, what turmoil has passed from the vagaries of life.

'ABDUL-RAHMAN JAMI, Iran's last great classical poet, described himself thus in his concise autobiography, *Rashah-i bal fi sharh-i hal* (The Exudation of Memory for Biography). Thanks to this work, and those of many other writers, we have a good picture of the life and character of this master of both Sufism and literature.

In the *Exudation*, Jami indicates that he was sent to school at an early age. After he gained sufficient experience in reading and writing, he began studying the Qur'an. Once he had learned and memorized the entire book, he continued with linguistics, logic, and philosophy. Then he undertook and completed mathematics, astronomy, and other subjects. Finally he mastered Islamic law, interpretation, and the Hadith (Traditions). In his words:

> From the science of Divine Law and its pillars,
> I knew the reason behind every commandment.
>
> From studying the Traditions, I became familiar with
> the Prophet's way and the methods of his companions.

However, the exoteric sciences were not enough:

> But my thirst was not satisfied with these sciences
> So I decided to apply what I had learned.
>
> I joined the ranks of the pure-hearted Sufis
> whose aim of studying is to become.

Jami does not indicate when he decided to be initiated, but apparently it was when he was still quite young. Moreover, he seems to have passed through the stages of development with remarkable speed:

> Remembrance and spiritual thought elevated me to the level
> at which the veils of Truth were pushed aside.

Jami tells us that after he reached a certain level of illumination, he was given the responsibility of composing poetry. He offers no further details of his life. Fortunately, however, many prominent people of the time wrote about him.

Jami was born in 1439 C.E. (817 on the Muslim calendar) in the district of Jam in the province of Khurasan. His birth came some five hundred years after Hallaj, who had lived in a very turbulent era. In Jami's century Sufism was well established, and many eminent masters such as Shah Ni'matullah Wali, Muhammad Nurbakhsh, and Baha'uddin Naqhshband had laid the foundations of some of the largest Sufi orders in Iran and India. By the time Jami was born, the invasion of the Mongols as well as the Tartars had taken place, and a relative peace had been established in both Persia and northern India. This break from warring times provided an opportunity for rebuilding Persia, in particular the capital city of Herat, where Jami spent most of his life.

King Shahrukh, a son of the Tartar invader, Tamerlane, and his wife were patrons of the arts and sciences, and especially of Sufism. In fact, there is a legend that whenever Shahrukh visited a city, he first visited the local *khanaqah* and its shaykh. As a result of Shahrukh's interests, Herat became a center of the arts and sciences. Thus, Jami was born in a flourishing society in which literature and the arts were at their height.

In a community of many learned scholars, Jami advanced to the top in a very short time. As a mathematician and scientist, he was revered by the scientific community, and the literary community praised him for his contributions to literature and poetry. As a result of his fame, a number of biographies were written about him. The following material is drawn from one of these — *Tadhkari Maykhana* (Memory of the Tavern), written by Qazwini in 1650.

It has been said that Jami's grandfather was one of the learned scholars of the city of Isfahan who moved to Khurasan and settled in the district of Jam, where Jami was born and from which he took his nickname. His father, also an educated man and the Islamic jurist of the district, moved to Herat when Jami was five years old. Jami began his studies with learning the Arabic alphabet under the direction of Junayd Ausuli and then attended the Nizamiyya School under the direction of Samarqandi. By the time he was fifteen, he had finished the courses that were offered. Because of his rare talents, he rose to a level that few had achieved.

He then moved to the city of Samarkand and continued his studies with Tabrizi, who was also the teacher of Agha Baik, the grand vizier of the time. This connection caused the eminent people of Samarkand to hear about him and admire his works. It is said that Abdul-Rahman Jami spent nine years in Samarkand, then left the city to return to Herat.

The biographers indicate he took a position with the school that King Shahrukh had built and began to teach. His fame was such that even Shahrukh's successor came to his lectures. It is said that Jami mastered every branch of the sciences of the time and wrote commentaries on them. His circle of knowledge included Sufism as well. In fact, he was held by many as an equal to 'Ibn Arabi, if not superior to him. Jami wrote a number of critical commentaries and explanations of portions of 'Ibn Arabi's *Fusus el-Hekam* (Jewels of Wisdom).

He seems to have lived in Herat until he was about sixty or sixty-four years of age, then left for Mecca on pilgrimage. There is a story that a number of people, who were sad to see him leave, told him that every good deed that he had done was equivalent to a pilgrimage done on foot (implying that the seeker had walked through the desert). He merely smiled and replied that his feet were tired of these journeys and he wanted to ride to Mecca for a change.

From Mecca, Jami left for Syria, then continued on to Egypt and Iraq and back to Herat. In all these countries, he was received with the highest honors and respect. He died at the age of eighty-one.

Qazwini does not offer any account of Jami's Sufism—except to say that he was good at it! One of his students, 'Abdul Ghafur Lari, related in a book titled *Taklameh* (Spoken Letter) that apparently Jami left Herat because he had developed a romantic interest in someone, and to rid himself of the desire he went to Samarkand and immersed himself in his studies. One night he was particularly sad thinking about his beloved when in a vision he beheld Sufi master Kashghari telling him, "My dear brother, go and find a lover that you cannot let go!"

The Beloved called from the Tavern, "Come,"
Then gave me the wine of love, cup after cup.

I rid myself of the shackles of logic and reason,
Then began to weep and cry for union.

After this vision, Jami was deeply affected and left for Herat,
only to come to Master Kashghari.

I saw a master under the blue heaven.
He was cleansed from his self like no other.
He was a mirror that reflected the Sun of Existence,
Reflections permanently shining in the form of a human.

In a relatively short period of time, he traversed the difficult
steps of the Path and reached a high level of perfection. In 1482,
Kashghari died and Jami turned to Khwaja Ahrar for further instruction and guidance. These two masters seem to have affected
him the most. There were others, but they were of much less
significance in Jami's life.

These two masters were of the Naqhshbandi Order. Jami men-
tions that when he was five years old he met Khwaja Muhammad
Parsa, who gave him a piece of rock candy. At the age of sixty Jami
could still remember Parsa's glowing face and the look of loving-
kindness in his eyes. Parsa was one of the most renowned masters
of the Naqhshbandi Order, and Jami attributes his inclination
toward the Naqhshbandi path to his childhood experience with
Parsa.

Jami lived a very long life. His disciple Lari describes his last few
days:

The number of years he lived was equivalent to the word ka's (in
the science of the letters of Sufism, every letter has a corresponding
number. In this way, letters were sometimes used as a means of
passing information only to initiates. The words ka's in Arabic and
jam in Persian both mean "cup." However, the word cup can also
be taken to mean that which holds the Divine wine of love and
knowledge. In other words, Lari may be referring to the high spiritual station of his master.

In his last year he had a vision about his time of departure, and very often he would recite the following.

> It is a shame that without us many days will pass,
>   The flowers will bloom and spring will come.
> Many summers, winters, and springs will pass,
>   and we will have turned into dust and clay.

A few days before his death, Jami began traveling to several nearby villages. One time he went to a village that he did not particularly care for; nevertheless, his stay became lengthy. His disciples, worried, rushed there. He told them, "We should cut ties."

Three days before his departure, he called some close disciples in and said to them, "Be my witness that I have no ties with anything or anyone." On Friday morning, at dawn, he felt the movement of the life force from his body. He stood to pray and then sat to attend to his litanies. By midmorning, he had departed.

A humorous story is told of the day of Jami's death. The Sufis, sad to see him about to depart this earth, had gathered at his house. Some were quietly weeping, while others were busy with their litanies. But one man was reciting the Holy Qur'an in a loud, harsh voice, disturbing everybody. Finally, Jami raised his head and said, "For God's sake, I will die if you don't stop that racket!"

Jami remarked on his own humorous nature in the following verse:

> It is better to be like lightning—bright.
> As long as you live, be happy and laughing.
> To bring a smile to a drooping heart
> Is better than giving away sweets.

A versatile writer, Jami left as his legacy eighty-one books on a variety of subjects. Among them are collections of poetry, an explanation of the works of 'Ibn Arabi, and *Haft Aurang*, a collection of seven stories in the form of *mathnawi*. Of these seven stories, his most famous among the common folk is *Yusuf and Zulaykha*, which we retell here in prose form. The story of Yusuf—the Islamic name for Joseph—is familiar to Jews and Christians from the Book of Genesis in the Bible. The Islamic version—told in sura 12 of the Qur'an and elaborated upon in Jami's poem—is somewhat different from the biblical tale. The episode about the attempted seduction of Joseph by his master's wife, called Zulaykha, here becomes a touching love story, in which Zulaykha's passion for the spiritually beautiful, virtuous Yusuf exemplifies the surrender of the human soul to the Divine Beloved.

YUSUF AND ZULAYKHA

At the beginning of creation, when all of Adam's future descendants were arrayed before him in a vision, he found himself drawn to one in particular, a man with a beauty beyond description. His face shone like the sun, his hair flowed down to his shoulders in curls, and his body was flawless in shape and form, like a tall cypress.

"Who is this man with such ravishing beauty that he casts a shadow over all the rest?" Adam in amazement asked the Lord.

"This is Yusuf," God answered, "the light of your eyes. He is the mirror of your heart, a flower from the garden of Jacob and Abraham. Cherish him."

Born in Canaan, Yusuf and his brother Benjamin were the last of Jacob's children, descendants of Abraham. He was the fairest of Jacob's twelve sons. In fact, his beauty could find no equal among humans, for God had revealed part of His own beauty in Yusuf. Because of this, everyone—young and old, woman and man—fell in love with Yusuf the moment they laid eyes upon him. Jacob was no exception. He loved Yusuf more than the rest of his children and could not bear to be apart from him.

In a land far from Canaan, there lived a king who had a daughter by the name of Zulaykha. So lovely was the girl that many willingly became her slaves just to be near her and serve her. The princess lived in peace and contentment, for her heart was untouched by others and her thoughts were free of worries and troubles.

One night, however, Zulaykha dreamed of a man seated upon a throne in a garden. She had never seen so handsome a man before: his face shone like the moon in a dark sky, his eyes were radiant as the stars, and his graceful body seemed like a work of art. One look at the man was enough to pierce Zulaykha's heart, sending a sharp pain through her body. Yet, it was as if she enjoyed the pain, for she could not take her eyes off the man.

In the morning, Zulaykha opened her eyes, smiling—until she realized that the beauty she had seen was only a dream. From that day forth, she found no peace in her soul, thinking of nothing but her beloved, wanting only to see the man in her dream. She spoke of him to no one. In her restlessness, she could not eat, and if she had not had the hope of finding her love in her dreams again, she would not have been able to sleep. Her once-rosy cheeks turned ashen, and her once-regal posture was bent under the painful weight of separation.

Finally, on a particularly bad night, after she had cried for hours and hours, praying that she might see her beloved again, Zulaykha dreamed once more of the man sitting in the garden. But this time, she approached him in the dream and told him of her love and pain, begging him to let her know who he was.

"I am the Grand Vizier of Egypt," the man replied, then suddenly disappeared.

Zulaykha awoke with a sense of calm and contentment in her heart. She sent for her maids, telling them to let the king know that she was once again ready to receive suitors.

When it was learned that the princess was receiving suitors, the kings of other lands began to send caravans to the palace with the most exquisite gifts and jewels in hopes of gaining the princess's hand in marriage. But Zulaykha rejected them all and continued waiting for the messenger she hoped would arrive from Egypt. This hope, however, was in vain, for no such messenger ever came. Eventually, unable to restrain herself any longer, Zulaykha had her father send a message to the Grand Vizier of Egypt, offering his consent to a marriage between Zulaykha and him. When she heard that the Vizier had accepted the offer, the young princess, now fifteen years old, was overjoyed. She set out for Egypt along with a great number of her maids and a treasure chest full of precious gems and pearls.

In anticipation of Zulaykha's visit, the Vizier had had a pavilion built for his bride-to-be just outside the city, for her to rest in before they met formally. But the princess was so impatient to see her beloved that she asked her chaperone to think of a way that she could have a glimpse of the Vizier without delay. Cautiously, the chaperone crept over to the Vizier's tent and tore a small opening in it; then she summoned her mistress. Upon looking through the opening, Zulaykha sighed and fainted away in shock.

"But this is not the man I saw in my dream," she exclaimed upon awakening—"The man in whose love I have lost my wits, the man who has stolen my peace and happiness!"

For hours Zulaykha wept and pleaded with God for mercy, wishing for her life to end there and then. Finally, a voice came to her from Heaven, saying, "The Grand Vizier of Egypt is not your heart's desire, but without him, reaching your goal will be impossible. Be patient, for you will soon gaze upon the beauty of your beloved by virtue of the company of the Vizier."

The news gladdened Zulaykha's heart. Wiping away her tears, she arose, confident of her future for the first time in as long as she could remember.

Yusuf had just turned fourteen. Shortly after his birthday, he had a dream. In the dream, eleven stars and the moon were all bowing to him in humility. When he told his father about the dream, Jacob advised him not to let anyone else know about it, especially his brothers, for the dream apparently foretold Yusuf's lordship over his eleven brothers and his parents. Unfortunately, Yusuf confided the dream to a close friend, who in turn told it to Yusuf's brothers. Driven by rage at Yusuf's arrogance and tired of their father's preferential treatment of him, they joined together to plot the elimination of their brother.

The next morning, the sons went to their father and asked permission to take Yusuf on an outing in the countryside with them. Jacob raised numerous objections to the idea, but the brothers insisted so vehemently that in the end their father agreed.

Once out of Jacob's sight, the brothers treated Yusuf with great cruelty. They beat him, tore the clothes from his back, and smeared his face with his own blood. Then they decided to throw him into a nearby well and leave him there, either to die or to be taken as a slave by any caravan that stopped at the well for water.

After three days, a caravan from Medina on its way to Egypt arrived at the well. When one of the travelers sent a bucket down for water, the angel Gabriel commanded Yusuf to get into it. Yusuf, who had been sitting forlornly on a rock, rose on hearing Gabriel's command and climbed into the bucket.

Upon sighting the approaching caravan, the brothers had hidden behind a bush, to see what would become of Yusuf. When they saw a man pull him out of the well, they approached him, claiming that Yusuf was a lazy slave of theirs and that they intended to sell him. The man, a merchant from the south who was struck by Yusuf's beauty, bought him for a few copper coins. Then the caravan loaded up and prepared to leave for Egypt.

Certain that Yusuf would never be able to get back to Canaan, the brothers stained his shirt with goat's blood and presented it to Jacob as proof that the boy had been killed by a wolf during a moment of their negligence. Meanwhile, the merchant who had pulled Yusuf from the well was preparing to auction him off as a slave in the bazaar of the Nile.

When the caravan arrived in Egypt, word soon spread that an incredibly handsome slave could be found among the Medinan caravan. People from all over came to the bazaar to see this reputed god of beauty. After seeing him, all burned with the desire to buy him. Many gathered up their life's savings to bid for him. Even an old wretched woman brought her only possession, some yarn she had spun. "This is all I have, but at least I can take my place in the crowd of buyers," she said. Enormous prices were offered, but not a single agreement was reached for his sale. For days, Yusuf stood on a wooden stage, dressed in silk, the radiance of his appearance dumbfounding those who caught sight of him.

Zulaykha was on her way back from a day of rest in the country when she heard the commotion in the bazaar. Asking a young man what was causing it, she was told that it concerned a Canaanite slave on display. As soon as the curtains of her carriage were parted for her to have a look at this slave, she cried out in shock and began trembling with excitement and mumbling incoherently. When her chaperone asked her what was wrong, she replied that this man was the one of whom she had dreamed so long ago, and whom she had loved ever since. Of course, Zulaykha set her mind on buying Yusuf. When she told her husband, the Grand Vizier, who had no son of his own, he welcomed the idea. And so Yusuf was soon purchased by the Grand Vizier and Zulaykha.

Needless to say, Zulaykha was not the only one in love with Yusuf. Another young woman, called Bazigha—a beauty in her own right, and wealthy too—had fallen in love with Yusuf just from hearing a description of him. Bazigha left her city for the capital, hoping to find Yusuf. The moment she saw him in the flesh, she collapsed. When she regained consciousness, she dropped at his feet, worshiping his majestic beauty.

Yusuf advised Bazigha thus: "When you see beauty and perfection in this world, it is nothing but a sign of Him. A beautiful creature is merely a single blossom from the vast garden of God. If you have the eyes to see the perfection, then you must also have the discernment to know that what you see is but a mirror reflecting the image of His face. My appearance, too, is a picture of God's own beauty. But you should know that a picture fades, a flower dies, and the reflection in the mirror is eclipsed by the real Light. It is He Who is real and remains so forever. In that case, why waste your time over something that is here today and gone tomorrow? Go directly to the Source without delay."

Bazigha replied, "Now that you have given me the secret, I can see the true Light. You have torn away the veil from my blinded eyes. Now that I can see the Beloved, I can love no other but Him, and I shall not rest until I am in union with Him. If every hair on my head could praise and thank you for awakening me, it would only be a small portion of the gratitude I owe you."

Bazigha said farewell to Yusuf and returned to her hometown. She gave away all her wealth, even her house and clothing. Wearing a coat of felt on her back, and eating only once a day, she resided in a cell on the banks of the Nile. Turning her back on worldly possessions, she spent the rest of her life in retreat, devoted to her Divine Beloved.

Zulaykha, on the other hand, was more than gratified at the turn of events that had brought her beloved to her. Ironically, from the day she had bought Yusuf, it was she who had become a slave to him, and not the other way around. She showered Yusuf with gifts—silken garments, jewelry, money—and spent all her time with him or thinking about him. At night, when he went to sleep, she would stay up, watching over him all night. But to her dismay, Yusuf's eyes never looked beyond his own feet or the designs in the carpet.

In an effort to ensnare Yusuf, Zulaykha began to tell him of her deepest feelings. With the sweetest words, she told him about her childhood dream and how the thought of him had never left her mind since that night, how her lips had said naught but his name.

"I am a slave to you and your husband," Yusuf replied. "The Grand Vizier has treated me like a son, and to him that is all I will ever be. So do not expect any more from me than being your servant. If, in fact, you feel as you claim, you should know that one whose heart is given to a friend thinks no longer of herself but loses herself in the wish of the friend. Her happiness lies in doing whatever the friend desires—and my wish and desire is to be a servant to you and your husband."

The more Zulaykha persisted, the more Yusuf resisted. Therefore, she decided to try a different approach. The following day, she sent Yusuf to a garden she owned. Among the trees, between two streams and flowerbeds where canaries and other birds sang, she ordered a bed be set for him with satin sheets and pillows. Then she chose a dozen of her prettiest maids, and prepared to send them to Yusuf. "I want you to serve Yusuf with all your heart and soul," she told them. "If he gives you poison, you should take it. If he sends you away, you should obey. But if any of you attracts his attention and desire, you must inform me first."

Should Yusuf be attracted to one of the girls, Zulaykha thought, she would switch places with the girl in the dark of night and deceive Yusuf into making love to her. Her efforts were in vain, though. The next morning, Zulaykha went to the garden and found her maids sitting in a circle around Yusuf, gazing at him in rapt devotion. As she drew closer, she heard Yusuf speaking of God and offering spiritual guidance to the maids, who had converted to the path of Unity.

In another scheme, Zulaykha's chaperone suggested building a new wing in the palace for Yusuf, with sensuous drawings on all the walls of him and Zulaykha embracing. Once he was forced to look at the pictures, temptation would enter his mind and he would eventually surrender to Zulaykha.

As soon as the palace was ready, Zulaykha put on her most exquisite dress and perfume, and sent for Yusuf. Indeed, she looked so beautiful that any man would have found her impossible to resist. When Yusuf arrived, Zulaykha welcomed him with a sweet smile, drew him into one of the rooms, and locked the door behind them. At first, she talked of her past and how her dream of him had driven her out of her mind. Yusuf kept his eyes fixed on the ground, talking of his loyalty to the Vizier and his wish to serve. Zulaykha took him through a doorway to a second room and again locked the door behind them. She told him of her devotion and of all the money and jewels she would sacrifice for him if, in return, he would only look at her. This time, too, Yusuf refused her. She took him to a third room, locking yet another door behind them. But Yusuf insisted that he would never betray his master or commit a sin.

Zulaykha took Yusuf through a total of six rooms, each time locking the door behind them, making sure that he would have no way to escape. In the seventh room, when she seductively tried to force him into looking at her, Yusuf turned his eyes toward the wall. There he saw a picture of himself in Zulaykha's arms. Stricken, he turned his gaze to the other walls and finally even to the ceiling, but everywhere he faced another love scene of himself with the Vizier's wife. Finally, he looked at her face. This lit hope in Zulaykha's heart. But Yusuf said, "There are two obstacles that prevent me from giving in to your wish: the first is answering to God, and the second is facing the Vizier."

"Do not talk to me of my husband," Zulaykha replied, "for compared to my love for you, he is nothing. I can poison him, or distract him from his ever knowing of our affair. As for your God, if He is as merciful as you claim, I will give alms and donations, and He will forgive us."

"You may very well hide your sin from the Vizier," Yusuf replied, "but you can never hide it from God. As for His forgiveness, was He paid for creating us, that He would now would accept a bribe to forgive us?"

Seeing that any further pleading would be useless, Zulaykha drew a dagger from her dress and threatened to kill herself. Yusuf pulled the dagger out of her hand and ran toward the door, fearing that unless he escaped, he might give in to her pressure. As he ran, each door opened in front of him as if by magic. Zulaykha ran after him, grabbing at his clothes. But she succeeded only in tearing the back of his shirt.

Outside the palace, Yusuf came upon the Vizier, who, noticing the young man's agitated state, asked him what the matter was. Yusuf invented a story, concealing what had really happened.

When Zulaykha saw the two of them talking together, she thought that Yusuf was telling her husband what had happened. She ran toward the Vizier, screaming and crying, claiming that Yusuf had tried to rape her, and demanding justice.

After an investigation had taken place, the Vizier realized that since Yusuf's shirt was torn from behind, someone must have tried to stop him from running away. He must therefore be innocent, since if he had been the attacker, the shirt would have been torn in the front. He had his guesses as to what his wife might have been up to, but to prevent any rumors, he decided to ignore the situation, hoping thereby to put the matter to rest.

The Vizier's hope was in vain, though, for rumor spread in the capital that the Vizier's wife had become infatuated with her slave. When Zulaykha learned of the rumors, she decided to shut the mouths of the gossipers once and for all. A short time later, she threw a royal banquet to which she invited all the ladies of the city. After dinner, the ladies were served oranges, and each was given a sharp knife with which to peel the fruit. At this moment, Zulaykha called for her servant Yusuf.

When Yusuf, more beauteous than the full moon, appeared in the doorway, one glance at him was enough to strike all the ladies dumb with wonder. So startled were they by his perfection that they could no longer distinguish the fruit from their fingers, and the tablecloth turned red with their blood.

After Yusuf departed and the ladies realized what they had done to themselves, they immediately understood the strength of Zulaykha's love for the slave and felt nothing but sympathy for her. They went to Yusuf and pleaded Zulaykha's case, but were no more successful than she had been. Returning to their hostess, they advised her to have Yusuf thrown into prison so that he might come to his senses and return her affection.

Ready to try anything at this point, Zulaykha summoned Yusuf and threatened him with prison if he did not obey her. He replied that he would rather languish in prison for a hundred years than give in to her demands. Frustrated beyond reason, Zulaykha went to her husband and convinced him to send the slave to prison, arguing that it would help to restore her ruined reputation.

After Yusuf was gone, how she rued her impulsive action, for now there was nothing more painful for her grieving heart than to find her beloved's place empty. After wailing for hours over her foolish mistake, she finally resolved to go to the prison to visit her loved one. At the prison, she asked the warden for a corner close to Yusuf's cell, a spot where Yusuf could not see her and she could watch him undisturbed. Hidden there, she found Yusuf in a state of meditative communion with his beloved God.

All night long she watched him. At dawn she returned home, but she found no comfort in her house. Zulaykha then moved to a room whose window overlooked the prison. All day long she would sit in a corner and stare at the building, far removed from the affairs of the world and even from her own self. She was close to only one thing—Yusuf. Day and night she mournfully poured her heart out to her absent love, and found nourishment for her soul in this practice. It became her only solace so long as Yusuf remained in prison.

In prison, Yusuf became a favorite among the other inmates. They found comfort and relief in his words and told him their innermost thoughts and dreams, so that he might give them advice and interpretations. Yusuf devoted himself to their concerns, taking care of the sick and relieving the sorrows of imprisonment.

One day, two of the previous king's courtiers who were serving time there told Yusuf their dreams. After listening to their dreams, Yusuf told one man that he would be hanged on the gallows, and the other that he would be restored to favor in the king's court. Eventually, their dreams came to pass. Before the man who was restored to favor left the prison, Yusuf asked him to mention his name to the king when he returned to court, but by the time the courtier was set free and had resumed his position, he had forgotten all about Yusuf and his request.

Years passed. One night the king had a dream that disturbed him greatly. First he saw seven lean cows attacking and devouring seven plump cows. Then he saw seven withered ears of corn twined around seven green ears of corn, destroying them. The next morning the king asked the sages of his court for an explanation of his dream, but none could interpret it. The king's question, however, jogged the memory of one of the courtiers, a man who had been freed from prison years before. He told the king of Yusuf's ability to interpret dreams. Upon hearing this, the king issued an order for Yusuf to be brought to him. To the king's astonishment, though, Yusuf refused to obey the order until he was set free, claiming that he had been unjustly imprisoned.

As a result, the king launched an investigation of Yusuf's supposed crime. When the ladies of the city were summoned to court and questioned about Yusuf, they all said they had seen nothing but nobility and piety in him. Then Zulaykha was called. Now purified of all her lies and treachery by the hardships of love, she confessed to her schemes and admitted the innocence of Yusuf.

And so, after years of confinement, Yusuf, now thirty years old, was released at last.

Presented to the king in the royal garden, Yusuf proceeded to interpret the king's dream. The seven fat cows and seven green ears of corn, he explained, represented seven years of good crops and prosperity, while the seven lean cows and seven ears of dried-up corn stood for seven years of drought and famine. The dream signified that for the next seven years Egypt would be rich in crops, while during the following seven years its lands would lay barren and fallow.

Impressed with Yusuf's ability, the king appointed him Grand Vizier, a position that had become vacant with the death of Zulaykha's husband. Given authority over the entire land of Egypt, Yusuf was told to do whatever was necessary to remedy the situation foretold in the king's dream. In response, the new Grand Vizier ordered that three-fourths of the crops harvested over the next seven years be set aside in storage.

During the years that followed, Yusuf was busy overseeing the plan he had conceived and taking care of the people's needs. In seven years, as he had predicted, famine spread over Egypt and its neighboring lands. Egypt, of course, was the only country with food. Gift-laden messengers came from all over, seeking grain and wheat. As it happened, one of the delegations was from Canaan and consisted of the eleven sons of Jacob.

At his palace, Yusuf received his brothers warmly but did not reveal his identity to them. The brothers bowed in homage to him, without suspecting that he was their own brother, whom they had abandoned in the well so long ago. Yusuf recalled his childhood dream and smiled. He then ordered that his brothers' bags be filled with grain and their gifts returned to them. In the bag of his youngest brother, Benjamin, however, he had surreptitiously had his royal cup hidden.

As the brothers were preparing to leave, the guards informed them that the royal cup had been stolen and that their bags would have to be searched. Eventually, the cup was found in Benjamin's bag. Yusuf, as Grand Vizier, ordered that the thief be held captive, as prescribed by law. The brothers begged him to take another one of them in place of Benjamin, as the boy was very dear to their father, but Yusuf refused. They had no choice but to return to Canaan without him.

Jacob, who had lost his eyesight from grief at his separation from Yusuf, could not bear the thought of being separated from Benjamin as well. He went into such a state of mourning when he heard his sons' news that the sons decided to return to Egypt and beg the Vizier to forgive Benjamin.

Yusuf, who had meanwhile revealed his identity to Benjamin, could not bear to see his other brothers in such pain and told them the truth, adding that he had long ago forgiven them. He told them to go back to Canaan and bring Jacob to Egypt, as it was no longer necessary for their father to suffer the pain of separation from his favorite sons. And he gave them his shirt to show Jacob that he was still alive.

When the brothers' caravan approached Canaan, Jacob stopped weeping—and when they gave him the shirt and he held it to his lips, he cried out with joy, for it held the scent of his beloved son. He is alive! Yusuf is alive!" Jacob exclaimed. Benjamin embraced his father and pressed Yusuf's shirt against his father's face. The moment the shirt of beloved Yusuf touched Jacob's eyes, his sight was restored. With his heart filled with gladness, Jacob set out for Egypt.

That heart which suffers on the Beloved's account is rendered dead to all other forms of joy and pain. No other sorrow clings to that lover's robe; no other happiness surrounds him. Let the world become a sea of affliction for him, with waves of sorrow as high as mountains: not even the hem of his robe will become wet. And if fortune were to prepare a banquet of eternal delights for him, he would turn his back on it. Nothing can distract him from his sorrow for the sake of the Beloved. — Jami[1]

Zulaykha had lost everything as the result of her love for Yusuf. After the death of her husband, she had abandoned her palace, finding her way to a ruined building, where she had lived in sorrow, crying incessantly and constantly repeating the name of Yusuf. During the first year, she had spent her last pieces of silver and gold in the hope of getting news of Yusuf; in the end, she had had nothing left to offer travelers for news of her beloved.

As the years passed, Zulaykha's youth faded. Her pitch-black hair turned to silver-white, her fresh, soft skin wrinkled, her slender body bent under the burden of her love, and her shiny black eyes were blinded by the tears she shed for her beloved. Though only forty years old, she looked like a woman of eighty.

Eventually, Zulaykha learned the route of Yusuf's daily travels and built a hut of reeds by the side of a road he used each day. Around the hut she constructed a reed fence, like a set of panpipes. As she sang her mournful laments of love, each reed would sound in sympathy with her. She lived in the hut, with only one hope — that Yusuf would notice her. Every day, when it came time for the Vizier to pass by, Zulaykha would rush out of her hut and sit by the roadside, waiting for her love. But as she heard the cries of Yusuf's guards announcing his arrival, she would fall down senseless. Later, she would regain consciousness and return to her reeds, singing her sad songs.

One night, Zulaykha knelt before the idol she had worshiped for years and prayed, "O you whom I have worshiped with devotion all my life, you who see my humiliation, if I cannot be with Yusuf, can you not restore my sight so that I can at least see him one more time?" Thus did she pray until dawn.

In the morning, when she heard the sound of horses, she ran outside. As Yusuf approached her, she shouted to him from the

depths of her soul. But her voice was drowned out by the whinnying of the horses and the shouts of people. No one paid the
slightest attention to her. Heartbroken, she went back to her
home. Taking a stone, she shattered her idol, crying, "You are
nothing but stone. Now I shall cast off your shameful domination
and be free of you once and for all. With the help of another stone,
I am going to smash the jewel of your power."² From the sudden
explosion that followed, she received a new light. She was washed
pure by her tears.

Earnestly, she prayed to God for forgiveness: "O Love, were it
not for the reflection of your image in an idol, no one would ever
worship it. Whoever bows down before an idol thinks that in doing
so he is worshiping divinity. O God, if I worshiped a piece of rock,
it was only myself that I wronged. Have mercy, and forgive me.
Let my heart be healed of the wounds of regret, and let me pick a
flower from Yusuf's garden. O Pure Being Who makes a king a
lowly slave and crowns a slave with the royal crown . . ."³

At this very moment, Yusuf happened to pass by. Hearing the
voice of an old woman lamenting, he was struck by its reverence
and ordered that the woman be found and brought to him in his
palace. When she was presented to him, he asked her who she
was.

"Don't you know me? I am the one who chose you over this
world from the moment I cast eyes upon you, who has loved you
ever since."

"Zulaykha? Is it really you? Oh, Zulaykha, what happened to you
and your beauty?"

"When I lost you, I lost them, too."

"What became of your cypress-like body?"

"Being parted from you was too heavy a burden for it to endure."

"And why have your eyes gone blind?"

"Deprived of sight of you, they wept tears of blood until they could no longer see."

"And what of all your wealth?"

"I gave my riches to whoever brought me news of you. Now nothing remains but my heart. And no wish do I have but to be able to see you one more time."

Astounded, Yusuf wondered why God had not ended this poor creature's life and spared her so much suffering. An answer came into his heart from the Lord:

"We have not taken her, for she has within her a whole world of love for him whom We love. Since her love for you is unceasing, We too love her for your sake. Who gave you the permission to seek the death of a rose in Our garden and to wish for the destruction of the friend of Our friends? Since she is filled with tenderness for you, how could you think We would take her life? Her weeping eyes bear witness to her love. Though for a lifetime We have driven her to despair, now We will make her young again for you. She has given you her own precious soul; if We now bless her, let her be to you as your soul."[4]

And by divine decree, Zulaykha's youth and beauty were restored. Her black eyes shone once more with light; her skin became radiant again like that of a girl of eighteen, and her loveliness was more ravishing than ever. There then came a divine order from God: "We now unite Zulaykha with you on the divine throne of marriage. So bind yourself to her with an eternal knot." A ray from the sun of Truth struck Zulaykha's eyes with such overwhelming brilliance that Yusuf was lost in it like a mote in a sunbeam. The lover and beloved were finally one.

The marriage of Yusuf and Zulaykha was a fruitful one, resulting in many children and grandchildren and years of peace and happiness for the two of them. Then one night Yusuf saw his parents in a dream. "O child," they said, "it is time for you join us. It is time for you to unite with us here."

In the morning, Yusuf told Zulaykha of his dream. Her heart was seized with pain, for she knew what it meant. That night, Yusuf prayed: "O Lord, do not leave me behind with the laggards; grant me a place among those who are nearest to You."

The next day, Yusuf went out riding. As he was about to place his foot in the stirrup, the angel Gabriel appeared to him, saying, "Your cup of life is now empty. Abandon the desire of riding the chariot of life and return to union with your Lord." Hearing this, Yusuf immediately gave up his soul.

At Yusuf's funeral, Zulaykha found the pain unbearable. Throwing herself on the grave, she uttered a final prayer:

"Oh, where are you now, Yusuf, to have mercy on the afflicted? You are hidden below the roots of a rose tree, and I am above like its flowering branches. You have slipped like water into the soil, and I am left on top like thorns and chaff. You have gone so far away that I can get no news of you from anyone. The loss of you sets such a fire in me that its smoke brings tears to everyone's eyes. I cannot bear to live without you."[5]

Pressing her wet face to the earth, Zulaykha kissed the ground in humble prayer and gave up her spirit as well. Her whole life, from start to finish, had been sacrificed to love.

If you know how to sacrifice your life, O reader, you have some conception of the secret of lovers that Zulaykha knew. But if you have no notion of sacrificing your life, all talk of the path and the goal will be of no avail.

"Lucky the lovers who, in dying, breathe their last with the aroma of Union in their nostrils."[6]

NOTES

INTRODUCTION

1. Javad Nurbakhsh, *Jesus in the Eyes of the Sufis* (London: Khaniqahi-Nimatullahi Publications, 1982), p. 98.

CHAPTER 1. A BRIEF LOOK AT THE HISTORY OF SUFISM

1. See N. Ardalan and L. Bahktiar, *The Sense of Unity* (Chicago: University of Chicago Press, 1973), and Seyyed Hossein Nasr, *Islamic Art and Spirituality* (Albany: State University of New York Press), 1987.
2. Idries Shah, *The Sufis* (New York: Doubleday, 1971).
3. Javad Nurbakhsh, *Divan Nurbakhsh: Sufi Poetry* (London: Khaniqahi-Nimatullahi Publications, 1980), p. 55. Reprinted by permission.

CHAPTER 2. HALLAJ

1. Louis Massignon, *The Passion of al-Hallaj, Mystic and Martyr of Islam*, trans. Herbert Mason (Princeton, N.J.: Princeton University Press, 1982), vol. 1, pp. 21–36.

CHAPTER 3. ABU SAʿID

1. Z. Kianinejad, *Rahe tasawuf dar Islam* (The Path of Gnosis in Islam) (Tehran: Eshraqhi Publications, 1987).
2. R. A. Nicholson, *Studies in Islamic Mysticism* (Delhi: Jayyed Press, 1976), p. 3.

3. Ibid., p. 5.

4. The author of *The Secrets of Unity* believes that Pir Abul-Fadhl died before Abu Sa'id finished his work and that Abu Sa'id received his cloak from Abu Abul-Rahman Sulami. Sulami's lineage was through Abul-Qasim Nasrabadi to Shibli and then to Junayd.

CHAPTER 4. ATTAR

1. Farid al-Din Attar, *The Ilahi-nama or Book of God*, trans. J. A. Boyle (Manchester: Manchester University Press, 1976).

2. There is an added section to this book that extends this work to many later Sufi masters, but it is not clear whether that is by Attar.

3. Adapted from Shah, *The Sufis*, p. 121.

4. Adapted from *The Sufis*, p. 122.

CHAPTER 6. RUMI

1. R. A. Nicholson, *The Mathnawi of Jalal'uddin Rumi*, vol. 1 (London: Luzac, 1977), p. 5.

2. Ira Friedlander, *The Whirling Dervishes* (New York: Collier Books, 1975), p. 40.

3. William C. Chittick, *The Sufi Path of Love: The Spiritual Teachings of Rumi* (Albany: State University of New York Press, 1983), p. 2.

4. Ibid., p. 3.

5. Shah, *The Sufis*, p. 151.

6. Dr. Javad Nurbakhsh, on page 25 of *In the Tavern of Ruin* (London: Khaniqahi-Nimatullahi Publications, 1978), defines Divine Love, or True Love, as follows: "In Divine Love the lover longs for the Beloved, not for himself, but only for the sake of the Beloved. . . . Temporal love arises from the beauty of transient forms. Like them, it is also transient—its only lasting result being the perpetuation of the species. It is the result of the sublimation and the refinement of sexual desire. Real or Divine Love, however, is a profusion and rapture from the Absolute Beloved which descends upon the heart of the sincere lover. This lover is like a moth that flutters around the

NOTES

beauty of the candle that is the Absolute, burning away its relative existence in His fire. The lover turns away from himself and perishes, inclines toward Him, and becomes alive. When the lover is emptied of himself and becomes nothing, he finds eternal life."

7. Adapted from Naser Sabebuz-Zamani, *Khate sevom* (The Third Script) (Tehran: Attaie Publications, 1989), p. 78.

8. In *In the Tavern of Ruin*, page 32, Dr. Nurbakhsh talks about *sama'* in the following fashion: "Though usually translated as 'spiritual music,' *sama'* literally means 'hearing.' In the terminology of Sufism, it is listening with the ear of the heart to music in the most profound sense—poetry, melodies, tunes, and rhythmic harmonies—while being in a special state so deeply plunged in Love that there is no taint of self left within awareness. In this sense, *sama'* is named the 'call of God.' Its reality is the wakefulness of the heart; its orientation is towards the Absolute. The Sufi in the state of *sama'* is not paying attention to either this world or the next. The fire of Love burns so intensely in him that everything but God is consumed. *Sama'* feeds that fire and gradually brings the Source of the sound and the listener closer and closer together until they become one."

9. Chittick, *The Sufi Path of Love*, p. 3.

10. Adapted from Sabebuz-Zamani, *Khate sevom*, p. 69.

11. Ibid.

12. Chittick, *The Sufi Path of Love*, p. 4.

13. Annemarie Schimmel, "Revisiting Mawlana Rumi and Konya," *Sufi: A Journal of Sufism*, , Winter 1988–1989, p. 7.

14. Quoted from *Mystical Poems of Rumi*, trans. A. J. Arberry (Chicago: University of Chicago Press, 1968), p. 5.

15. Nicholson, *The Mathnawi of Jalal'uddin Rumi*, vol. 1, p. xiii.

CHAPTER 7. JAMI

1. *Jami: Yusof and Zolaikha*, trans. D. Pendlebury (London: Octagon Press, 1980), p. 116.

2. Ibid., p. 121.

3. Ibid., p. 122.
4. Attar, *The Ilahi-nama*, trans. Boyle, p. 297.
5. *Jami: Yusof and Zolaikha*, trans. Pendlebury, p. 135.
6. Ibid.

GLOSSARY

'ALI   The Prophet Muhammad's son-in-law and cousin, who was the fourth caliph after Muhammad. The majority of Sufi orders trace their lineage back to 'Ali. He is also a role model for many Sufis in that he was the first to traverse the stages of the spiritual path under the guidance of Prophet Muhammad and reach the station of the Perfect Human Being.

BAQA'   The attainment of divine characteristics and being sustained by God; the stage after *fana'*.

BAST   A feeling of spiritual happiness given to a Sufi by God; expansion of the station of a Sufi's heart.

CINCTURE   A belt worn by Christian or Zoroastrian monks. In Sufism it is worn as a sign of devotion; it is also a symbol of service to the master and God.

DERVISH   Literally, an impoverished person; today it refers to a seeker who has been initiated into a Sufi order.

DIVAN   A collection of lyric poetry.

DIVINE LOVE   A strong attraction and force that drives a person to search for Truth. Also, the force that separates the Sufi from the world of multiplicity and brings him or her closer to the world of Unity. See also note 6 for chapter 6.

FANA'   The annihilation of human characteristics in God.

GHAZAL   The best-known form of Persian poetry, consisting of a short poem of ten to fifteen stanzas, with monorhyme and the rhyme scheme aa xa xa xa xa, etc. Love is the theme of many *ghazals*; another common theme is the expression of the spiritual state of the poet.

HADITH   The "Traditions" of the Prophet Muhammad, consisting of extra-Qur'anic accounts of his words and deeds, collected and recorded by his followers.

HAJJ   Pilgrimage to the Ka'bah in Mecca, which is a religious duty to be undertaken at least once by every Muslim.

HAL   Literally, the present moment. To Sufis, *hal* refers to the impression of the Divine that enters the heart. It also denotes an ecstatic state.

HAQIQA   Truth; the destination of someone who follows the spiritual path (*tariqa*).

JINN   An invisible being endowed with magical powers. The common belief is that jinns are demons with hoofed feet and goatlike faces. Some believe that the jinns also seek God, just as humans do, and that, like humans, they have both good and evil individuals among them. There are many accounts of Sufi masters having jinns as their disciples.

KA'BAH   A black cubical building in Mecca that symbolizes for Muslims the house of God. It is the goal of a Muslim's pilgrimage, and the direction toward which Muslims turn when praying.

KAF   A legendary mountain located at the end of the world and impossible to reach.

KASHKUL   The begging bowl carried by dervishes to show their spiritual poverty. Today, it is generally used as a symbol of spiritual poverty at the *khanaqahs*, or Sufi centers.

KHANAQAH   House of Sufism, the place at which Sufis hold their spiritual meetings. Historically, newcomers would go to the local *khanaqah* if they did not know anyone in town.

KHIRQA   A mantle or cloak worn by a Sufi. It generally has the connotation of authority.

KHIDR   An immortal Sufi master, described in the Qur'an, who may appear in different places to guide aspirants.

MADRASA   A school or theological college.

MATHNAWI   A style of narrative poetry, consisting of rhymed couplets and generally used either to tell stories or to present discourses. Rumi's famous epic poem, the *Mathnawi*, is named for this style.

MECCA   A city in Saudi Arabia; the goal of a Muslim's pilgrimage.

NAFS   The ego; the lower self; the part of the psyche that identifies with the self. The Sufis generally identify four types of *nafs* on the spiritual journey to God: the commanding *nafs*, the blaming *nafs*, the knowing *nafs*, and the *nafs* at rest.

NAMAZ   Muslim prayer.

PIR   One who guides travelers on the Sufi path toward God.

QABD   A feeling of spiritual sadness given to a Sufi by God; the station of contraction of a Sufi's heart.

QASIDA   A kind of poem very similar to a *ghazal*; however, it is much longer and generally tells a story or has a specific lesson to teach.

QAWWAL   Literally, a singer. The one who sings at a spiritual gathering (*sama'*) of dervishes.

QIBLA   The direction in which Muslims face when they pray, that is, toward the Ka'bah in Mecca.

RAK'AH   A division or part of the Muslim's daily prayers. A Muslim daily prayer consists of seventeen *rak'ahs*.

SAMA'   Literally, "listening." In Sufism the term refers to the act of intense and ecstatic listening and meditation to the accompaniment of Sufi music. Sometimes it evokes involuntary movements of the body, resulting in *sama'* dancing, or Sufi dancing. See also note 8 for chapter 6.

SHARI'A   Divine Law; Islamic canon law.

SHAYKH   An Islamic title given to one who is qualified to guide seekers on the spiritual path. Sometimes it refers to a Sufi master.

SILSILA   Literally, a chain; the lineage of masters of a Sufi order.

SUFI   Dervish; one who is initiated into a Sufi order; a seeker who by means of love and devotion moves toward God.

SUFISM   A spiritual way of reaching God through the gateway of the heart by means of love.

TARIQA   The spiritual path of the Prophet Muhammad; Sufism.

VIZIER   In old times, a vizier was the king's consultant. Today, the term refers to a cabinet minister.

WUDHU'   Ablution; the ritual of washing before prayer or pilgrimage.

ZIKR   Remembrance; a practice whereby a Sufi initiate remembers or chants one or many names of God, as directed by the master.

ZOROASTRIANISM   An ancient Persian religion, founded around 600 BCE by the prophet Zoroaster (or Zarathustra), with a belief system based on the existence of a supreme deity, Ahura Mazda, who created both good and evil. Ahura Mazda calls upon people to follow the principles of good thoughts, good words, and good deeds.

BIBLIOGRAPHY

ENGLISH

Arberry, A. J. *Mystical Poems of Rumi.* Chicago: University of Chicago Press, 1968.

'Attar, Fariduddin al-Din. *The Ilahi-nama or Book of God.* Translated by J. A. Boyle. Manchester, England: Manchester University Press, 1976.

———. *The Conference of the Birds.* Translated by C. S. Nott. Boston: Shambhala Publications, 1993.

Chittick, William C. *The Sufi Path of Love: The Spiritual Teachings of Rumi.* Albany: State University of New York Press, 1983.

Friedlander, Ira. *The Whirling Dervishes.* New York: Collier Books, 1975.

Massignon, Louis, *The Passion of al-Hallaj, Mystic and Martyr of Islam.* Translated by Herbert Mason. Princeton, N.J.: Princeton University Press, 1982.

Nicholson, R. A. *Studies in Islamic Mysticism.* Delhi: Jayyed Press, 1976.

———. *The Mathnawi of Jalal'uddin Rumi.* 3 vols. London: Luzac, 1977.

Nurbakhsh, Javad. *In the Tavern of Ruin: Seven Essays on Sufism.* New York: Khaniqahi-Nimatullahi Publications, 1978.

Pendlebury, D., trans. *Jami: Yusof and Zolaikha.* London: Octagon Press, 1980.

Schimmel, Annemarie. "Revisiting Mawlana Rumi and Konya," *Sufi: A Journal of Sufism,* Winter 1988–1989.

Shah, Idries. *The Sufis.* New York: Doubleday, 1971.

Shusud, Hassan. *Masters of Wisdom of Central Asia.* Translated from Turkish by Muhtar Holland. Oxford: Coombe Springs Press, 1983.

Sufi: A Journal of Sufism. London: Khaniqahi Nimatullahi Publications.

PERSIAN (FARSI)

'Attar, Fariddudin. *Ilahi-nama* (Book of God). Tehran: Maharat Publications, 1988.

———. *Mantiq al-tayr* (The Conference of the Birds). Tehran: Maharat Publications, 1987.

———. *Tadhkerat al-awliya* (Memoirs of the Saints). Tehran: Markazi Publications, 1957.

Eghbal, 'Afzal. *Asare Mawlana dar farhange islami* (The Effects of Mawlana on Islamic Culture). Translated into Persian by Mohammad Rafi'i. Tehran: Attai Publications, 1983.

Este 'llami, Muhammad. *Hallaj.* Tehran: Amir Kabir Pubications, 1972.

Jami, 'Abdul-Rahman. *Divan Jami.* Edited by Hashem Razi. Tehran: Pirouz Publications, 1964.

———. "Yusuf wa Zulaykha," in *Haft Aurang.* Tehran: Amir Kabir Publications, 1969.

Kadani, M. Shafa'i. *Halat wa sokhanane Abu Sa'id Abul-Khayr* (Words and States of Abu Sa'id Abul-Khayr), 2nd ed. Tehran: Agha Publications, 1988.

Kianinejad, Z. *Rahe tasawuf dar Islam* (The Path of Gnosis in Islam). Tehran: Eshraqhi Publications, 1987.

Massignon, Louis. *Masu'eb Hallaj* (The Afflictions of Hallaj). Translated from French by Zia'uddin Dahshiri. Tehran: Foundation for Islamic Sciences Publications, 1982.

Mubasheri, Asdollah. *Chang-e Mathnawi* (Mathnawi's Harp). Tehran: Attai Publications, 1983.

Nizami, Hakim. *Khosrow va Shireen.* Edited by V. Dastgerdi. Tehran: Elmi Publications, 1964.

———. *Laily va Majnoun.* Edited by V. Dastgerdi. Tehran: Elmi Publications, 1964.

———. *Sharafnameh.* Edited by V. Dastgerdi. Tehran: Elmi Publications, 1964.

Qarib, Farid. *Wudhui khun* (The Blood Ablution). Translated from Arabic by Bahman Ruzani. Tehran: Mawla Publications, 1980.

Qazwini, Mulla 'Abdulnabi. *Tadhkarat maykhana* (Memory of the Tavern). Edited by Ahmad Gawlchin Ma'ani. Tehran: Eqbal Publications, 1988.

Sabebuz-Zamani, Naser. *Khate sevom* (The Third Script). Tehran: Attaie Publications, 1989.

Sabur, Salah Abul. *Sugnama-e Hallaj* (The Eulogy of Hallaj). Translated from Arabic by Baqer Mu'in. Tehran: Amir Kabir Publications, 1978.

Safa, Z. *Asrar-e tawid fe magamate Shaykh Abu Sa'id* (The Secrets of Unity in the Stations of Shaykh Abu Sa'id), 4th ed. Tehran: Amir Kabir Publications, 1981.

Zarinkub, A. *Arzesh miras-e sufiyya* (The Value of the Sufi Heritage), 5th ed. Tehran: Amir Kabir Publications, 1983.